VAMOS!

The Avon Plate Story

Searching For The Soul of Sunday Morning

Neil Boulton

Order this book online at www.trafford.com/07-1723
or email orders@trafford.com

Most Trafford titles are also available at major online book retailers.

Note for Librarians: A cataloguing record for this book is available from Library and Archives Canada at www.collectionscanada.ca/amicus/index-e.html

ISBN: 978-1-4251-4170-7

We at Trafford believe that it is the responsibility of us all, as both individuals and corporations, to make choices that are environmentally and socially sound. You, in turn, are supporting this responsible conduct each time you purchase a Trafford book, or make use of our publishing services. To find out how you are helping, please visit www.trafford.com/responsiblepublishing.html

Our mission is to efficiently provide the world's finest, most comprehensive book publishing service, enabling every author to experience success. To find out how to publish your book, your way, and have it available worldwide, visit us online at www.trafford.com/10510

www.trafford.com

North America & international
toll-free: 1 888 232 4444 (USA & Canada)
phone: 250 383 6864 • fax: 250 383 6804 • email: info@trafford.com

The United Kingdom & Europe
phone: +44 (0)1865 722 113 • local rate: 0845 230 9601
facsimile: +44 (0)1865 722 868 • email: info.uk@trafford.com

10 9 8 7 6 5 4

Author's Acknowledgements

The author wishes to thank all those who helped make this book possible. My wife, for putting up with my disappearing for hours on end as the story became an obsession. Thanks to The Plate for the inspiration. Many thanks also to: Nick Jump for the book's cover design, to Cris Sherratt & Sandra Cooke for the photographs and to Yos and Daz for keeping me sane during frustrating IT technicalities.

For my children.

Introduction:

Christmas time, mistletoe and whine-ing religious crackpots such as Cliff Richard and his ilk. A time of trepidation, for opening the gifts that will strain your acting skills to the max, 'Oh lovely, just what I wanted, how did you know?' and the smile that starts to hurt and look like a pained grimace. Imagine my glee then, as a red-blooded male who is bang into his footy, whether watching on the telly-box, devouring football-related literature, playing on a Sunday morning, or chatting ad infinitum about it in the pub, to receive a copy of 'Any Chance of a Game, the ugly side of football', this was obviously good news. This is a rare tale of hopelessly low-level football and the feeling was that it would make a refreshing change from reading about the professional game which is 99% like reading the latest 'Hello' magazine (not that I ever would, unless in a waiting room): concentrating on the celebrity and looks of the preening-pros with a small and grudging observation of the actual football being played. I was looking forward to the amusement of shared experiences and thoughts and the absurdity of the lengths one goes to for the sake of a game, beautiful or not.

Now, Barney Rogan's book is a damn fine read, and when you are starved of the sort of subject matter this covers, it was read very quickly and enjoyably. The recommendation would be to give it a read if footy is your bag. However, I was left feeling a little short-changed as there seemed to be little love for his team, not much desire to actually be playing the game, and Mr. Rogan relates how he was near retirement even though he was only Thirty odd and his niggles are nothing compared to the creaking and aching of my 39 year old bones. Thus, Mr Rogan is to be thanked by myself (and hopefully others) for inspiring and motivating me to write this journal of this latest Avon Plate FC season and my part in it.

I would also tip my hat towards Gary Nelson and his books: 'Left Foot Forward', and 'Left Foot In The Grave'. These are his diary-type works of his time as a final-year pro at Charlton Athletic and as Player-manager at Torquay United. Again, these books are about the lower ends of the league, albeit still a lot higher than Avon Plate. If, as I do, you enjoy a good tale of inconsistency, injury, brutality and the clinging on to football playing, then that is why I am offering this Plate tale to the public.

Another inspiration is my wife who is currently studying astrology. She has made a statement based on the fact that Avon Plate will be in its tenth season of existence this time around. Apparently this is a half-cycle of the moon's nodes. Nodes are connected with destiny and our full potential. "Challenges to meet and rise to, unless one's destiny is to be a failure". So glory, or glorious failure is nigh. Should be interesting. As a further comparison to 'Any Chance of a Game?' it made me laugh that the author was having to reconcile playing footy with having a girlfriend. I don't know yet, but my having a non-football-loving wife and three children under five years old may also turn out to be a bit of a dilemma too.

I feel the need to clarify some thoughts with regards the passages dealing with my marriage. Our relationship was young and we were going through a rough time. I have tried to represent the situation as it was, in my head, with all the misunderstandings and issues that were unresolved at the time. This book charts the journey from my decidedly warped view of things, through to a greater understanding of myself, my wife, and, possibly, life in general. This is in no small way thanks to the patience, love and understanding of my wonderful partner and I cannot thank her enough for what she has done for me. I can only hope that seeing the process, as it was for me, in black and white, is not too painful for her (would you allow your partner to read your diary?) but only shows the long journey that I needed to take. Thank goodness it was with her.

It is to be hoped that the spirit, love, commitment, passion, highs & lows, skill, failure, fun and frustration that usually accompanies 'A Season With The Plate', will shine through. Along with the trials and tribulations on and off the pitch, if a picture, of how unique an experience it is to play for a Sunday League football team that you cannot do without, arises, then my job here will be done.

The Plate:

We were formed as a team in the summer of 1997. The offspring of our now honorary el presidentes' James Masters and Dan Thomas (whose names deserve to be in print for this achievement alone). We are not a works or a pub team, but the hardcore are a group of mates who got to know each other through connections we built up whilst studying at Bristol's University of the West of England. Once the partying and general avoidance of going onto campus was dealt with at the end of our degrees, we realised that we shared a level of fitness of not even being able to run for the bus. We also shared a love of the beautiful game. Thus, for once being able to actually organise something through the dope-smog, Avon Plate were entered into the Bristol Civils League. A 10 team, 1 division, lightly organised league.

The name comes from our desire to be a cross between the South American philosophy of football (keep the ball on the deck, be passionate about your team, look pretty) and the more British philosophy (hoof it under the least pressure, use lots of football clichés whilst shouting, fair play, energy will make up for shortfalls in technicality, no compromise of lifestyle). Hence, we tend to display an up and down game of stylish patterns mixed in with atrocious self-destruction. Our kits are lush. Home is White with red sash a la River Plate and our away kit is the Blue and White stripes a la Argentina (you can only imagine the attempted kickings we take after world cups, especially 1998 and the Beckham/Simeone fiasco). Still, that is what is to be expected, other clubs do tend to raise their game against us because we look so great and are brittle at times (especially in the period in-between when the ref blows his whistle to start, and then stop, a game).

The famous Plate spirit was formed in this initial three-season period. We were consistently hammered by double figure tallies. Our record defeat was at this time, a 13-1 defeat to our fiercest rivals: Woodland Road. Other teams, like the Bristol version of Sheffield united; Blades, used to love playing us with a great deal of 10 goal plus hauls, although we used to take the mick out of them as they used to just stick to what was successful for them and never try anything new. Sure, 'if it aint broke don't fix it' but hoofing it up the middle for larger –than-average blokes to crash into and feed off the second ball, well, it's not my cup of tea or idea of an enjoyable time, certainly isn't when you are on the receiving end. Plate developed the tendency to latch on to any rays of hope and become deluded mightily easily as to what we could realistically achieve and aim for. Also, a knack of wearing rose-tinted glasses when reviewing our performances in the pub afterwards. A healthy 'never say die' attitude was fostered.

The ease of which we accept into our fold, any player who shows any signs of knowing what they are doing on a pitch, has also been very helpful. Plate players also blatantly think the world of each other and this rubs off on those unfortunate enough to come into contact with us and get sucked into our universe.

Once we had found our feet, could raise a team of 11 on most Sundays, had finances under control, were no longer morbidly unfit, and newcomers to the game (we now knew vaguely what was expected in an 11-a-side match), we applied for and joined the Bristol & District Sunday League. I must admit, this switch was heavily influenced by my pressure, I was the oldest in the team back then and wanted to experience the thrill of relegation / promotion and cup competitions before I had to retire.

The following six seasons have been a roller coaster ride of 1 actual (last season) and 2 near relegations, 3 mid-table obscurities and 1 glorious promotion year. Possibly our greatest feat was achieved in 2000 when we actually won the Charles Finch Cup at Hallen FC, we were newcomers in Bristol & District division 5 up against a division 1 side. I believe that they weren't expecting such a low-level team to be as fired up and ready for it as we were, I certainly don't think that the 90% Plate-crowd were expecting anything other than a drubbing from the opposition, but that is football, and 120 minutes later we were tear-stained heroes. The only blow for me was that I had torn cruciate ligaments in my right knee during the final pre-season game of that year and was therefore manager on the sidelines. There was a degree of satisfaction and achievement but I can still only pray that I get one last chance to actually grace the pitch in a big match with crowd and proper referee and assistants on a lush, flat pitch.

The Build up:

The Plate squad as we approach the big kick off is:

Yos / my best mate / fellow hairband wearer / poached with much glee from fierce rivals Woodland Road / short of sight but long on footy prowess / apparently has the look of Harry potter about him which may explain why he grew his hair and then cut it again when Harry had flowing locks for the 'Goblet of Fire' movie / social secretary / striker

Dr / Mr reliable as long as someone else has organised a wake-up call, a lift, his kit, some cash for a pint or two after / original Plater / would nine times out of ten win the man-of-the-match award if the rest of us didn't acknowledge his skills and then ignore them in favour of someone else who has kicked the ball almost exactly where they intended, sometimes / striker

Jumpy / Man Utd glory seeker which partly explains why he joined us lot / penalty-taker extraordinaire and set-piece maestro / training secretary / full back

Jerry / Placid and calm and difficult to wind up, but when you do, watch out / takes no prisoners / manager / centre-back

Sherry / unlike the above, easier to wind up that a clockwork toy that has a smooth wind up action as its unique selling point / new age (pikey) hair dos / the anti-epitome of consistency / cannot run / Sunday money and stats secretary / goalkeeper

Simon / oldest Plater (41 this season) / on joining, told us he had trials with Aston Villa and I, for one, believed him which just goes to show how crap Villa have become these last few decades / getting more into the Plate the older he gets / centre-back

Drew / original Plater / usually 'almost fit' or 'just about over an injury' / default shirt-of-shame vote winner / cannot ref as is too easily intimidated / has ball skills 'issues' amongst many others / most likely to enlighten you on his sexual exploits, no matter how little you want to hear them / if asks where the toilet is, run for it, can stink-out a changing room within nano seconds / he gets a mention in this section simply because we have all known him so long, and heard so many intimate stories, that I couldn't possibly leave him out / centre midfield

DJ James B / bears the brunt of most of my in-game shouting / would struggle to be beaten in a 'wildest shooting' competition / techno-geek who runs the Plate website / winger

Dan / Co-founder member / Tallest Plater / Went out on loan to a London club for a season to learn his trade and came back much more 'savvy'/ Honorary 'el presidente / Almost as tall as Peter Crouch, with roughly the same heading ability / Centre back

Reg / Original Plater / Destroyer of teams, unfortunately, some of the time it is our own team (usually but not exclusively at training sessions) / brother of Dan and therefore involved in a great deal of the bitching which usually starts between the two and has to be nipped in the bud before the rest of the Plate are distracted and embroiled / initiator of the 'Wrong Ray Award', given for the biggest foul-up of the season (i.e. texted a guy called Ray-a semi pro keeper- 'yes' is the reply from Ray, we turn up for the match and it is a ray who has never played before) / centre-midfield

Ga / Fellow Ram / never fails to be amused when he realises yet again, that he is older than me by a few months / Once given a Bi-Polar Disorder diagnosis so can presumably play down both flanks at the same time / winger

Joff / American 'soccer-ball' player / local music 'star' with his ukulele / brave but generally in no state to feel any pain / emergencies-only 'keeper

Lewis / after many 'will he wont he show' comments, seems determined to show he is committed and has this Sunday morning thang covered / winger

Craig Davies / pronounced a la Bo Selecta / only his third season for us but is already a stalwart, always at training, comes to watch when injured etc / winger

Lee / 'don't you know I'm a policeman', shout has shown how low the cops are considered in modern people's minds / feels like a brick wall if you try and go round him and your trick does not work / leaves committing to a match to the very last moment / centre midfielder

Ross / 'use in extreme emergency' / reserve goalkeeper

Daz / 1st full season for the Plate / has some mental health issues as is a Forest fan / as likely to put in the perfect through ball as he is to air-kick / tough as old boots & as strong as their smell / left back

Louis / newcomer to the squad after joining in the middle of last season / one of group of young 'uns / loads of energy (needed with the rest of the ageing Avon Plate old-guard) / already a first-team choice / left midfield

Korahn / chum of Louis / seems to be some sort of semi-pro skateboarder-type-dude / gnarly player / as one young filly quoted, he is 'as fit as f*ck' / right midfield

Dave / used to play in a team, years ago, with Jumpy and Lee and is in his 1st season with our lot / has already shown a feisty side in training / seems to want to be committed in training, coming along every week, and coming to the pub after, which is always nice / centre back

Ali / this chap joined us in our training sessions over the summer and quickly decided he wanted to sign up / know little about his play and personality / attacking-type

Bolts / and then there is me. As I am the player I know the best, I get a bigger entry. An original member of the Plate, I was honoured that on my return from a travel in Thailand (that had turned into quite an ordeal) I found that my name was down for the Plate. So I hadn't been forgotten and I really needed my friends at that point so, as I say, well chuffed.

I had played almost every day at junior school (at the time I was living in Nottingham but, as it was 1975, the majority of the footy team supported Derby county and I have followed them ever since). In those days we had a set number of assignments to complete in week, in maths etc, but once you were in the footy team then the number of assignments was very low. In the mornings we would pick the lunchtime teams. Lunchtime, we played a game and in the afternoon we chatted about how the game went. At the weekend we would play for the school team. Oh for the days when teachers were not only passionate about sport and so on, but they had the time and the flexibility of curriculum to see it through. Since adulthood though, I had not really been a participant of exercise. By the time we entered the Bristol & District league I think I was fit and playing centre midfield better than I have experienced before or since. In the final pre-season game, my right knee turned over and was agony. I played on for a few more minutes but my knee was twisting and jarring me with pain every time I went off a straight line. My cruciate ligament had snapped. Unfortunately, it was misdiagnosed at the hospital and then by a physio who kept treating it for medial ligament damage. Worse, he was telling me to play on and train my brain for the pain. However, every time I tried to play it turned over horribly. Thus my role that season was as manager. We had arguably our most successful season. Plate won the Charles Finch Cup and finished a respectable mid-table in the bottom division of the league.

I have a medal, memories and photos but I have the dream to play in a proper cup final before I have to retire. 'New Labour' had still been following the pre-set Tory spending plans, so it took about 18 months before my knee was scanned on the NHS. The consultant told me that my ligament had re-attached itself to a part of the inner knee that was not where it had originally come from. I was assured that it would be strong enough to play on without an operation. I do still play, and try to play every game in the season if possible. The knee turns over once or twice a game but it doesn't hurt at the time and is only slightly achy after the final whistle. It also turns over when I'm gardening, or playing with the kids and times when it catches me out 'cos it feels as if I'm not doing anything like as strenuous as footy. It seems that if I pull on the knee at the wrong angle it goes. Since I can play on, I wont think of an op until I pack the football in.

After the injury I found that centre midfield was too much for me and so I went to right back in a vain attempt to help shore up our leaky defence (averages about 3 goals per game against although it is usually similar amounts with goals scored). I am usually arguing to get back to a more advanced playing position, I used to score 10 a season when in centre-mid, when fit (rare), I like to think of myself as a rampaging full back and tend to end up with around 2 goals a season nowadays.

The Plate has become more important to me since I got married. At that point I took on boy/girl twins, marrying their mother when they were 18 months old, they are now five and we have since added Louis to the fold (now 2). So football has become my way of keeping up with a large proportion of my good friends. I never had a large group of great buddies until I moved to Bristol at when I was 25, so they are like my family really. Also the footy gives me release from family life. I don't profess to be a 'natural born father' and need 'me time'. It is great for me to have Thursday evenings out with training, pub, Yos' house, and then Sunday day with match, pub, home. My wife was not at all into football when we met. She is not really into football now. She has been to see me play a few times and brought the kids along when possible. It is quite a seperate thing from her though and it can get quite hairy when a lot of Plate holidays, meetings/ parties come up at once. Usually I leave telling her of most planned things until the last minute, which exacerbates any problems. After the last trip away (I had taken my 1st week away with the cricket team, and then a few days away with the footy team) it did get to the point where we had to think about whether we really wanted this marriage to work. Once I had knocked down the walls of the little room in my head, where I had locked my emotions, it was immediately clear that I didn't want to lose my marriage and the family. So, as a gesture, I have agreed that this will be my last season as club secretary (I also, will not be going for the offered cricket team captaincy). My wife does a lot of organising to help me keep up my full-on relationship with Avon Plate whilst having a young family to bring up.

Playing for the Plate obviously makes me happy which gives me the reserves to carry on when things seem all too much. My job certainly doesn't help with giving me energy to carry out all my duties in life. I am a housing officer in the field of mental health. I support people who are in danger of losing their tenancies without support, have had a chaotic life in the past, and have mental health issues. All sorts of mental health and personality disorders to contend with. Inappropriate housing, neighbourhood disputes, financial woes, inability to deal with authority, court fines and appearances, setting up and maintaining support networks, reducing isolation, family relations, children, partners and exes, government department foul-ups, low-level counselling, its all there and more in my job. If the caseload weren't quite so large, I would really love my work. With meetings and training and 'team-building' plus mountains of the usual bureaucracy, it leaves me a little pushed to actually see and work with the actual clients. As it is I am good at it and it gives me a measure of enjoyment with a hell of a lot of satisfaction and achievement, and tiredness in my own brain. The theory being, that certain people are classed as having, 'Personality Disorders', and they offload their feelings onto their support worker, leaving them as angry, impatient and frustrated as the client feels.

I am club secretary. Seven seasons in the job, partly because no other bugger wants the responsibility, and also because I appear to be bloomin' marvellous at it. The league hasn't fined us for 4 seasons, we haven't postponed a match for 4 seasons, and I won the divisional secretary award 3 seasons ago and won the 'Cliff Bennett Memorial trophy' for being the best secretary in the whole league last season. Myself, and the others on the Plate Soviet, relish our roles as leaders of the Plate and we sit on the top table at the agm where we dish out the awards, give motivational speeches, and make the underlings feel they are making democratic decisions in the forward planning of the Plate. After all this time though, and the aforementioned decision with regards my wife and family, plus the general decline in Plate fortunes of late, means it is not so hard to move on from that role.

I wouldn't dream of playing for another club.

The Non-Player Resources:

After nine years, at the end of last season, we lost our 'spiritual home'. Quaintly titled 'The Bush' (as in the Bush Resource & Activity Centre). We lent the keys, and thus the pitch to a Casuals League team. It was at the end of last season. We had, as usual, finished early because The Bush was a miracle pitch that never got called off due to the weather. Eventually, this other team wanted to play a match and the council had taken down the posts. Their secretary then rang the office of the Bush and demanded that the nets were put up. Of course, the management of the Bush had no idea who they were and weren't at all happy that we had lent out the facilities without their knowledge. As the place is owned by Social Services, they have been looking for a way to get us off so that they can sell the land. Health and safety was the reason given for our removal. I then had to stop giving cricket 100% of my thoughts, and instead, concentrate on finding us a new home. Not easy given the state of teams to pitches ratio in the 'City of Culture', Bristol. We have finished up with a berth at the Cadbury Frys sports facility in Keynesham. I am pleased because we no longer have to sort out the pitch before the game: unlocking changing rooms, putting out corner posts, putting up the nets, taking everything down again, cleaning the changing rooms and locking up. Another benefit will be that the pitches at Frys will get called off if the weather is really bad. Our squad will not get so tired and stretched by having to play every week (due to the Bush's aforementioned special quality). A downside is that Frys costs twice as much as the Bush used to so this season we are a bit strapped for cash.

We have also had to look for a new sponsor. The pub that sponsored us last year has changed hands and the new owners are too busy gurning and being 'The Oldest Ravers In Town' so they blew it with us. So we take our business, our followers, our pictures off the wall and leave them to fend for themselves. Fortunately, The Greenbank pub is also under new-ish ownership, so the landlord needed to build his new public house empire. As a great start he decided to accept the Plate into his life. Although he seemed slightly 'out of it' when we chatted, it seems that food and love will be on offer to us and that is all we really want. A welcome, some chat with the staff, our pints pulled in quick time, and a home that loves us. Money has not been mentioned yet although Tony (the landlord) seems keen to get us a new kit (typically, the only thing we don't really need is a new kit, the Argentina one we use for change kit and the River Plate one we use for rest of matches still look bloomin' smart. We tend to be the best-looking club in Bristol (and that certainly includes Bristol Rovers with their shocking pink kit). Let us hope that Tony and the Greenbank works out better than our last sponsor deals. The landlord at the Old England pub ended up going a bit mad and upsetting our team until we had to leave (a great shame for me as I had had our evening reception do there for my wedding and it was a brilliant time. Guard of honour at the door, great 'club-type' set up in there), tons of memories in our 5 year or so link up (win or lose, always on the booze, fights, girls, dodgy food, post-match-post-mortems etc etc). Last years' pub landlord never got round to doing us food and the landlord was incredibly hard to track down when it got to sponsorship money time. So, this year, I was on the case with finding new sponsorship (another distraction from the cricket and my family. Thus, exacerbating the compartmentalising of my life and the detachment from those I really couldn't bear to lose). I chatted to the new landlady of the Old England pub. We were in negotiations with a drinking establishment in Clifton (expensive beer, lots of university students), which I could never get the hang of the name, The Bon Bon Arena or something. It was Tony though who said the most right things and that was decided.

The social secretaries of the Plate Soviet did their best this summer. They managed to keep the spirit going via the traditional, yearly camping trip, as has become custom, to Parc-Le-Breos down Gower way. This is a site owned by the Scouts. There are bugger all facilities, including no toilet or washing on site although there is a heritage site up the road where you can freshen up if that takes your fancy. In the main we just to get more and more out of it and so the dirt becomes less of a problem. It also makes it difficult for families to attend, especially when, like mine, you have three young 'uns in tow. Plus, if your wife isn't that keen to expose the kids to a group of tokers it doesn't become any easier to integrate them. On the plus side, fires can be built and there is usually bugger all other campers around so we can be as raucous as we like. Amazing what a load of alcohol, various combustibles, home-made fireworks, beaches, ball-games, hugs and the like will do to bond humans, especially a football team.

Occasionally, there have in the past been those members of the squad whose job it is to wind up as many of us as possible. However, following the 'Night of the long Tony's' a couple of seasons ago, this problem has vanished. A guy I introduced to the team, scored five goals in his first game and then became the most arrogant and destructive member of the squad. Every match we would be wondering when it would kick off between Tony and the opposition. Eventually, it got to the point where we could not be bothered to want to protect him anymore as he was causing us as much grief as any opposition. The people he was introducing to us were also not really the kind we were after: crack and other substance abusers. The types who would be out of it on a Sunday morning, shouting and screaming at the other team and their supporters. Stuff we really did not need to be honest, Sunday mornings are usually filled with enough angst as it is. One of his 'chums' also had it away with a years' worth of Plate surplus funds and ended up as a star of the local rag after a hostage situation involving a machete. The end for Tony came when a large section of the team threatened to quit and so it was left to me to break the bad news. As well as being a bit of a pain, Tony had another side to his personality that was generous and friendly and loyal and avoiding. Thus, he was shocked and stunned by the reaction of the Plate and it took several difficult, awkward and diplomatic conversations before he accepted the inevitable and left.

Pre-Season Build Up:

Well, I say 'build up'. This summer has been incredibly lax on the whole. We had a couple of months off, whilst the World Cup was on. As an ex-manager myself, as well as player and fan, I feel I must have my say on Sven. I felt he was not brave enough for the job of England manager in a tournament situation. Although Hargreaves has come on in leaps and bounds, the sight of him starting against Trinidad & Tobago made my heart sink. It is a statement of intent that would have made our opposition grow in confidence. They would see us protecting ourselves, rather than as an attacking, exuberant team who were going to make their lives hell for the next 90 minutes or so, especially as he then allied that choice, with playing a 4-5-1 formation. The final curtain on top of all this was Sven seemed to have no plan 'B's and when he did make substitutions, they would leave you scratching your head more than before. Not all players need a manager that is shouting and screaming from the sidelines. Erikson's lack of passion/motivation/instructions, from the sidelines was too much the other way. Footballers aren't really grown-ups when they are on the pitch. They want adulation. They want to hear, from the person it matters from most (the bloke who picks the team), how great that pass was, or to be told, 'They are just hanging on, go and finish them off....brilliant!' Anyway, enough of that for now. As he is still appearing in the press regularly, I may come back to the 'waster of the golden generation'.

So, we had the break from playing, watched the matches, got inspired and got back to training. Where was everybody though? Eastville Park, Thursdays, 6.30pm. Only about 8 of us there. This continued for weeks. I was deep into my cricket season, and, having decided to quit as club secretary at the end of the season, was feeling a bit bitter about having to do any footy organising at a time when I should be thinking only of my opening-bat efforts and putting my footy kit in a bag and turning up. We managed to get Dave, and then Ali involved which was a boost. However, none of the young 'uns from last season had turned up, no contact either. With only a week to go before the season began, Louis emerged, signed up and said he had spoken to the other young 'uns and they were up for it too. Can't count on them yet because we haven't seen them, but it meant that we seemed to have a squad of 24 players. By the eve of the season, we had lost three players: Alex (centre midfield), couldn't keep up playing Saturdays and Sundays, we lost out. He had a good footballing brain to run things from the centre of the park. Drew retired. We shall miss him very much.

He will still get honourable mentions down the pub, plus votes for the shirt of shame (most embarrassing moment of a game), I'm sure. One of the young 'uns: Tyler, had started a family and I get the impression we won't be seeing him for a while. Ross and Joff were also clear on them not playing unless it was a dire emergency. Squad looking a bit threadbare now. Last season we had far too many games with bare 11s or worse showing up for Sunday's games. Will history repeat itself?

Last season was painful. We started badly, got worse, had a mid-season surge which then tailed off terribly and we ended up relegated as the 3rd from bottom side. Our record was dismal: Played – 18, Won – 6, drew – 0, Lost – 12, Goals For – 37, goals Against – 74! Our lack of numbers was the key to our downfall. Comedy 'play' at times of the worst Sunday morning type including: air kicks, afraid of the ball, weak in the tackle, not coming back to defend, profligate in front of goal, giving the ball away in front of the defence, little communication and what there was tended to be mostly arguing amongst ourselves, defending corners and set-pieces was a lottery, unfit and old as a team.

With that sort of form behind us, it will take hard work to turn it around. Unfortunately, with me not putting in my usual effort, and the manager being one of those who couldn't make training (childcare), it meant we did not get it together to play any pre-season friendlies, at all. On a selfish note, I couldn't make friendlies on a Sunday because of cricket matches so didn't try my hardest. Thursdays were too poorly attended to arrange a proper match. We were left with discussing tactics, whilst in various non-sober states, and playing beach soccer on the camping trip. When I think back to our cup-winning year, we had a full-on pre-season. Fitness work, ball skills, loads of warm-up matches. With this summer's preparation, or lack of it, plus the low feeling following relegation, the shrinking squad and our approaching middle ages, it does not leave me with a great sense of optimism. Twenty-two tough league games and a number (probably very low) of cup games approaching. I will refuse to listen to any voice of reason though. Yet. I am a hell of a daydreamer. Can do it for hours a day easily (usually aided by the marijuana-induced state that I more often than not find myself). I am still having the odd one where Plate win trophies and I score 20 goals or so. Hope will thus spring eternal(ish).

Sunday 3rd September 2006

Avon Plate versus Warwick

Frys Club Bristol & District Sunday League Division 4

Team:

Sherry

Jumpy Dan Jerry Daz

Bolts Reg Lee Craig

Yos Dr

Sub: Ga
Ref: Tim (not league appointed)

Our first home game. I am therefore a little distracted as I am hoping the rest of the team share my enthusiasm for our new home. Bad start as we have been allotted the smallest changing rooms and even though we only have a squad today of 12 players, it is a squeeze and gives players the chance to have a grumble. This can happen on Sunday mornings and can sap spirit. I would hope that the grander facilities and the fact that everything is done for us pitch-wise, will galvanise us. The pitch does look great. The nets are up and corner flags are out, another worry over for me. The next distraction is the ref. There is no league ref assigned to us (a very common thing in this division). So I have lined up a work-mate of mine who plays for a Casuals League team, but is not playing today. Frys is also his team's home pitch so he knows where it is but he is still a little late and has no whistle or linesman's flags. So, I am having to run around assuring everyone that a ref is coming. I then have to borrow the ref's kit off the Warwick secretary. Finally I can think about the game.

Warwick were relegated with us last season as they finished 2nd from bottom. We played them 1st game last season and they beat us 2-1. They have a lovely bloke as their secretary, I believe he was once on the league committee and is almost certainly a well-known figure in the local amateur footy scene. Just like last season, they asked me to countersign some player registration forms so that they could play some new players. Usually, one has to wait 7 days for a registration to take effect. Last season they dropped off and we beat them in the return game. I reckon that their secretary can get new players in, as he is a man in the know, but then cannot hold onto them for whatever reason. They have a large squad in size and numbers today. More than us for sure. The gleaming white with red sash Plate kit does piss all over their yellow and blue number.

I had a chat with their secretary about the referee situation because he has clout and is an approachable guy. As teams, we pay the same amount to affiliate to the league as the Premiership division teams, as well as the all the others. Referees are always assigned to the top leagues and down, so when you reach division 4 there aren't enough to go round and we end up with no ref. Not fair we cry. Joint action to be taken, possibly in the form of stern emails or similar. It is having a referee that makes a game 'proper' as opposed to a kick about in the park. The local newspaper coverage (The Bristol Evening Post, not world renowned. Results and fixtures plus the odd match report in 'Game of the Week') and the website, the league meetings, the cup competitions are all fine and worth paying for. The referee allocations need to be more evenly spread though it must be said. There are quite a lot of reserve teams in our league, it often gets annoying because you never know which team we are going to face. Their actual reserves or mainly first teamers? So, get rid of reserve teams, have less matches and more proportion of games-to-refs. This must be a problem all over the country. Leagues will just have to bite the bullet and take less money, or charge more to the surviving teams. Aren't the various FAs supposed to have millions swilling around? Having this guy, Tim, today is good because at least he isn't a member of either of the playing teams and knows about football, he isn't aged or overweight either.

We play a straight forward 4-4-2 formation. Even so, we look rusty and like we haven't played together for months, which we haven't. Daz does several air kicks, Jumpy and me are struggling to get much going on down the right, but what crosses and passes we do get in is more than the left from where there is nothing. Reg looks dazed. The boys up front are 'working hard'. Dave at the back is getting irate. For the 1st time ever I hear an Avon Plate player inform his opponent that he will 'nail him'. Dan is having an absolute 'mare. For such a tall lad, and with several seasons of playing behind him, his heading and positional sense and just general centre-back-type toughness are all missing. As usual, it does not take long before the brotherly love of the Thomas' turns to arguing and Dan going into sulky-head-down-mode. All in all, we go three down in the first half hour. At this point I really notice the stiff wind we will be playing into for the second half and my heart does sink a little.

The second half turns out to be as much hard graft as I imagined, but we were also far less in the game as I imagined we would be. Sherry's goal kicks are practically going backwards and we cannot get out of our own half. Jerry made the only change that he could: Craig for Ga with 20 minutes to go but we continued to crumble. 8-0 loss. What a dreadful start. We were never at the races. We capitulated like Avon Plate of 10 years ago. I was so little involved that I am tired from running but have no new bumps, bruises, strains etc. Only physical sign of play is that the left big-toenail that I damaged whilst opening the batting in the summer has come off. The right big-toenail is starting to turn its usual blue and will fall off just before the cricket season starts next year. Oh, and a couple of blisters from wearing studs on the dry end-of-summer pitches.

The ref is paid his £20. An easy game for him. We had a game last season that wasn't so easy. The league game against Merryweather kicked off with one of their guys doing the refereeing. It was our home game but we had no one on the sidelines that believed they were a competent ref. Within 10 minutes, the ref's own team had turned on him, calling him all the names under the sun, questioning all his decisions. As we began to play them off the park, Merryweather's behaviour deteriorated so that at half time, their guy (turned out to be a goalie of theirs) decided he wanted to play the second half and not ref any more today thank you. Up stepped Ga. As far as I remember, we were 4-3 ahead and Merryweather were desperately pillorying Ga at every turn. Ga began to crumble and gave them a penalty for nothing really. This still wasn't enough for them. Football had pretty much gone out the window in favour of organised clattering. We began to lose our shape and cool and went behind. They seemed hell bent on injuring Louis but he stood up for himself and finally, they fouled him once too often and Yos started some argy-bargy with their skipper. Scuffles break out all over the pitch but nothing to compare to their goalie, bouncing from his goal line into our half and jumping on Ga. With no choice, Ga has to abandon the game with Merryweather ahead with about 2 minutes to go. With all the minutes spent by the league about the sanctity of referees, we have still not heard anything from the resulting GFA investigation and the incident happened about 6 months ago now.

As instructed, we had a drink in the rather splendid, but no smoking indoors, social club at Frys. Then it was onto the Greenbank. To top off a not-so-splendid day, Tony the landlord was not about, neither was any food, nor any welcome or hint of recognition from the barmaid. Beer was thankfully on tap and

it was a roof over our heads. One of the rituals we look forward to (especially Sherry with his computer-designed forms and love of stats) is the voting for the 'Shirt Of Shame' and the 'Man Of The Match' awards. Each player has to vote, they can't vote for themselves and there should be a reason given. The Shirt is for the worst or most comedy moment of the game, Man O'Match is self-explanatory. The season's first awards went to:
Shirt of Shame: Dan (shouting at Reg)
Man of the Match: Yos (worked hard)

After the jovialness of that, I began to get a bit irate and wrote a stinking letter on an envelope, which contained a catalogue with some green kits in for the landlord to peruse. I put that it was 'rubbish', and 'no good', that I had 'turned down other pubs', 'do you want to sponsor us or not?' etc. The boys advised me to not give it to the barmaid for him and that we would work on him over time. I was pissed off thinking back to the past couple of landlords and couldn't be hacked with putting up with any nonsense any more. Small changing rooms, no league ref, no food or welcome, who do they think we are? Don't they realise how lucky they are to have Avon Plate associated with them? Wont anyone love us like they should? So I did hand the note in, and then fret about it for most of the following week.

Training on Thursday at Eastville Park was as useless as ever. Only a 4-a-side game was possible. Eventually, skipper Yos got angry and was having a right pop at us for playing, 'Pitter Patter' football. He was having no more of it and gave us a lecture on having to play tough on Sundays. Do the dirty jobs. No half-hearted nonsense. Get a football-head on for the new season. We continued the chat down the pub afterwards. The conclusion to be drawn was that we didn't ever want to beaten in such a whimpering way and with scores of 8-0. It would be too soul-destroying. The only thing to lighten the load was that Tony had left me a phone message. He was desperately sorry for not being there on Sunday but he had been too busy. He asked what sort of food we would be after and promised he would sort it out. Although I didn't ask him to, he provided a sumptuous array of sandwiches on that Thursday night and gave me £275 cash for a new kit that we can then put the Greenbank logo onto. Back to Yos' house after the pub with Ga. A long session of Tokeing and talking. We thrashed out what we thought was wrong with the Plate. We decided that we should put all the most regular, committed, strongest and consistent players in the middle. This bunch would not concede possession under pressure, would give the spine of the team a good understanding and make us more solid so no more capitulations a la Warwick. Jerry, Simon, new Dave, myself, Yos, Lee and Dr would now form the centre backs, centre mid, and centre forward positions. It would mean switching to one up front. The balance of the squad means that most of the new, young or periphery players could now battle out for the wide positions, meanwhile the centre would be more secure we hoped. I emailed Jerry the next day. I expected him to move me into centre back as I am supposedly one of our best defenders. Usually, Yos and I play 'Total War' on the computer for hours before I struggle back home across town, no time this week with all the lovely Plate chat. Fingers crossed we can start to work it out on the field of play or I can only see woe and maybe even the end of the Plate.

Sunday 10th September 2006

Farmhouse versus Avon Plate

Kelston Close, Yate
Bristol & District Sunday League Division 4

Team:

Sherry
Jumpy Dave Jerry Daz
Bolts
Ga Yos Lee Louis
Dr

Subs: Ali (for Ga, 80 mins)
James B (for Jumpy 45 mins)

As a team, we cheer each name as Jerry calls it out. When he called my name in central midfield, I couldn't help but give an extra loud holler. It has been so long that I have been picked in what has always been my favourite position. In the Makelele role to boot, what an honour. Jerry has certainly gone for the strong centre option and with Reg away, and out of form, it gives me my chance. Yos and Lee have, between them, high work rate, football brains, skill on the ball and don't mind getting stuck in and doing the ugly stuff. Going 4-5-1 (or 4-3-3 however you look at it) is a bit of a gamble as it takes us into Sven territory, but we do have a much better manager.

The first joyous job of today's event is to witness the two teams clearing the pitch of broken glass, which is embarrassing for them, the council, and the idiots who put it there. Eventually, we are all happy enough and their bloke blows the whistle.

It soon becomes apparent that we have suddenly become a solid unit. Confidence spreads throughout the team. Whether Farmhouse come up the wings or through the centre we have them covered. As the half wears on I am feeling the connection you get with the game and that central position. You can sense the rhythm of the game, it ebbs and flows. Once you get really good, you can begin to alter the tempo of the game seemingly by yourself. Although nowhere near that yet, I am seeing things happen before they develop into danger. I am getting a thrill out of just breaking up their play.

With a few minutes to go in the half, Dr gets the ball on the edge of their penalty area. As usual, he holds onto the ball for an age. As Farmhouse are tiring, I am able to take a chance and bomb up field. Because I'm not around their box much, the Farmhouse defence don't pick me up. I scream at Dr to pass, again but louder. Finally, the ball is rolled out to me, the closing down begins but too late. I have caught it beautifully with my left foot. It dips, bends and smacks into the bar and post before hitting the back of the net. My celebration consists of getting Yos to stand in front of me whilst I head butt his chest. I think Zidane would have been proud of the goal but not the head butt. Yos and Lee are providing an excellent shield in front of me; the communication behind me is excellent. We are all over them when they get the ball and smothering all their threat. Daz looks transformed. Jumpy looked in good form until an ankle knock forced him off but his replacement, James B, was straight into it. With someone like the Dr playing the lone front man, we may have stumbled onto something. He tends to hold up play anyway, his style of dribbling rather than passing gives us a chance to get up and support him and he is an excellent out-ball. Louis is a constant threat with his pace, energy and dribbling skills. It is he, who opens the scoring today. Nice and early which helped settle any nerves. It is absolutely fantastic to be on the other end of the situation where the massive gap opens up in the centre of the park. This time the gap was in front of me and I could actually run with the ball from defence and set things going. 2-0 is a proper football score too. This result couldn't have come quickly enough after last week. It was such fun too. Absolutely knackered after the game but my knee had stood up to midfield rather well.

A win and the Greenbank has prepared food! Our cup runneth over.
Shirt of Shame: Dr (wearing an old pair of slippers instead of boots)
Man of the Match: Bolts ('left foot edge of box beauty')
Obviously, my day is made. There is much rejoicing and the decision of the pub to sponsor us looks a good one if today's takings are anything to go by. We tend to live by the maxim' Win or lose, always on the booze', but after a good win there is less effort involved in the early stages. Ga is proving himself to be the Greenbank table tennis champion.

Finally, this week sees a useful training session as we play the Easton Cowboys in a friendly at Eastville Park We play our new formation, have 13 players turn up and manage to draw 1-1. They are top of division 2 at present so we are feeling fine.

I know the common perception of mental health is that it is something you are stuck with forever, that one is dangerous or erratic, it is a contagious disease, these people are a drain on society, why did Thatcher close the mental hospitals and let them roam the streets? People like my mother find it difficult to even listen when a conversation takes place about what I do. I believe she still thinks I work with children in some capacity. Well, working in Learning Difficulties for Five years *was* very soul-destroying. The way it didn't matter what money was spent, how and which activities are set-up, you end up going round in circles. With mental health, I have seen success and I want to see if it continues. Three years into the job and I am wondering how long I can keep in this 'industry' as it must surely burn me out at some point. Most days will see hours of low-level, 'every-day-talking' counselling through to deeply depressing, chaotic and abusive scenarios. As the support worker you end up taking away, from meet-ups, a lot of the client's emotional baggage. This characteristic is common in many 'Personality Disorders'.

I came into the job with only life-experience. I had no previous work experience with this client group although learning difficulties is packed with mental health issues but are just not given that label. My life-experience was a hell of one though so I didn't feel completely out of water. Plus, my project deals with people who have made the first steps of getting their own, independent tenancy, so we have a head start.

Client issues at work, at the moment include: supporting someone to get over an accident at work (that has robbed them of self-worth and confidence leading to depression, drug use, anxiety and paranoia.), debt work, relationship breakdowns, uncontrolled Diabetes, a teenager out of prison, acquired brain damage, hearing voices, alcoholism and re-housing due to harassment.

Sunday 17th September 2006

Oracle versus Avon Plate

Muller Road, Horfield Evening Post Cup Round 1
Ref: S Saunders (league appointed ref)

Team:

Sherry
Reg Simon Jerry Daz
Bolts
Ga Yos Lee Louis
Dr

Subs: Craig (for Daz, 60 mins)
Ned (for Louis, half time)
James B (for Ga 70 mins)

Oracle are an old foe of ours. We seem to have been in the same division as them for goodness knows how long. They came down with us last season from the 3rd division. We usually win and lose each season against them. This is quite a difficult game to prepare for. If you lose the 1st round of this cup competition, you are then entered into the Charles Finch cup. As we have far more chance of winning the Charles Finch, we tend to lose this match and play all the fringe players and the new players. However, after last week, we are determined to get a winning run going and we see the need to try and get the new formation bedded-in. Thus, we are going to go for it. We have an actual referee and a full squad of 14 players, plus we know on our day we can beat this lot.

The match proves to be a great test of the formation. Oracle are now strictly a long-ball team. Even when they picked up possession in our half they would lump it forward. Trouble was, they had a very good and very tall bloke up front but if the ball ever got to him he was laying it off to nobody. The other forward they had was quite good, but was very Heskey-like in that he seemed to fall over constantly. We found that in the main, either I would cut out their long ball or it was easy meat for Jerry and Simon and Sherry has decided to boss his box more, so anything that got past the rest of us was mopped up by him. Their only goal came from a mishit clearance that was whacked by their guy and it flew into the top corner. Other than that, the near clean sheet was secure. Meanwhile, we were making hay with our own possession. Apart from Louis doing too much trickery in his own half and giving us palpitations. The Dr had one of those days with a blistering 4 goals of which some could easily be termed net-busters. 4-1 to the Plate.

Two wins on the bounce. It obviously wasn't luck last week. The only downer is that we will draw a shit-hot team at some point and that may not be such an enjoyable match to play in although I am sure we shall see the funny side down the pub after. Another bonus was that after the match, we were shaking hands with the opposition, as you do. I noticed this guy called Tom had been playing for them. He works at the same support agency that I do. He had grown a sort of beard and had obviously kept a low profile as we wiped the floor with them. So, I didn't recognise him in the heat of battle. We have a Derby County / Southampton footy rivalry at work. It was glorious to puff out of breath, 'and we dicked you today'.

So to the pub after. No Tony and no food again. This time it is a snotty text from myself to himself. The moans and groans of the team don't last too long thanks to the good mood of the win. It

was nice to have Simon around for his banter and dry humour. Nice to have the young 'uns around as they are interesting for their attitudes and human beat-boxing and generally being fresh and really into the Plate. Louis and Ned seem to have a good mix of skating, music, partying, being cool and managing to be committed and regular football team members. A slight downer is that Jumpy had to miss the match due to the ankle knock he took last week but he says he'll be over it soon and we seem strong enough to cope with the odd injury absence at the moment.
Shirt of Shame: Reg (breakdance throw-in)
Man of the Match: Dr (prescribing goals like only the Dr can)

A benefit of the cricket season is that my wife has got used to me getting in late on a Sunday. So after the pub it is back to Sherry's for Sky Sport's. 'Grand Slam Sunday'. Thrash Metal and explosions abound. Andy 'Too Much Heading Has Made Me This Way' Gray informs us, 'Put simply, if Liverpool or Arsenal lose today, their season is over.' Chelsea beat Liverpool 1-0. Man Utd Lose 1-0 to Arsenal. However, Liverpool are still 2 points ahead of Arsenal and there are fully 7 months of the season left, so how truthful is Mr. Gray's statement? To make matters worse, I watched the Liverpool match with Yos and Sherry using the new-fangled system: Sky Plus. This is hailed as a subscription service that offers a personal video recorder. Fully integrated with a Sky digital decoder. The system apparently uses an internal hard drive. It allows the user to record, pause live television and instantly rewind. Unfortunately, the system broke down about an hour into the match, which, I am afraid, dulled the whole Grand Slam Sunday experience.

Sunday 24th September 2006

Avon Plate versus Brislington 1987

Frys Bristol & District Sunday League Division 4
Ref: (Peter of the Commercial & Friendly league)

Team:

Sherry
Reg Dave Jerry Daz
Bolts
Ga Yos Lee Ned
Dr

Subs: Simon (for Ga 64 mins)
Tony (for Lee 80 mins)
Ali (for Ned 80 mins)

Unfortunately, it seems that the '1987' in their team name is their average year of birth, as they all look very young and fit. Not only is it old versus young, but also they are wearing the Brazilian gold and green kit versus our Argentinean River Plate kit. Also unfortunately, on this occasion they play slightly more like whom they look like than we do. To make the match even more professional looking, the referee I have managed to book, looks and acts the part. Yet again, we have a lovely day for it and a full squad to choose from.

Lee and myself are at each other's throats almost straight away. As has happened many many times throughout Plate history is that when we have won a couple of matches we think we are the best team that ever lived. Lee is playing as a striker and not bothering to chase back. I have words but, as can be the way, he takes everything as a personal attack on himself. It annoys me that with most players, you shout something at them in the heat of the moment or with some tactical advice, and they get all bloody defensive and try and lay the blame for anything at the door of someone else. I want my teammates to shout at me. If I have done something really shit, I will hold my hand up and take the flack and determine not to do it again, not just start pretending I was perfect and affronted that someone may say otherwise during a football match.

Anyway, they were the first team that has played three in midfield as we do now. Instead of covering the spaces around the defence, I was now sucked into a man-to-man marking situation. Not so much fun as it takes away my periodic moments of attack. Perhaps our downfall was masked by the fact that we went 1-0 up with a cracking goal from Dr. I had played the ball into the channel for Ned to reach at the by-line. From there he pulled it square on the ground for Dr to knock in from 6 yards. By the time we realised that we should be 3 on 3 in the centre, and that Lee was not a second striker, we were 3-1 down and feeling deflated. At 2-1 down I had also put a cross in, on the run, with my left foot, which fell to Ga about 1 yard away from goal and central. Somehow he missed it. From then on we weren't in it. We didn't crumble. When Simon came on for Ga we were briefly lifted and pulled a goal back with a super strike from Lee. It was hard to take thought that our recent resurgence had been stopped, albeit by a seemingly very good, young, fit team. We scored one more consolation via the Dr but final score: 3-7.

Tony at the Greenbank says he doesn't want to be associated with losers. At the moment I don't feel quite like that but, just in case, I hope he was joking. Food is on the go with sausages in gravy and roast potatoes. It seems it is either nothing, or far better than we expect / deserve. After much gnashing of teeth about a seemingly backward step. We finally calm down and the view seems to be that we are still getting used to the change in formation and we cannot expect to be consistent yet. Spirits are raised with the votes:

Shirt of Shame: James B (falling over kitbags as he ran the line, 2nd season in a row for this occurrence)

Man of the Match: Lee (solid stuff)

Sunday 1st October 2006

Northville Athletic Reserves versus Avon Plate

Ashley Down RFC Bristol & District Sunday League Division 4

Team:

Sherry

Ga Reg Jerry Jumpy

Bolts

Ali James B Lee Ned

Louis

Sub: Craig (for Ga 79 mins)
No league appointed referee

Northville are a team that has evolved into a big club. Their first team is way up the divisions and we played against them before they got a reserve team together. They trounced us then but they are not setting this division alight yet. I do recognise some of them. Today is the first really dirty weather of the season. It has been storming and raining all night and all morning. As we arrive there is such a downpour (one of many) that we couldn't get out of our cars. I had been expecting the call all morning that the game was off. I had loads of texts and calls to reply to assuring my blokes that the game was on and they should get out of their warm beds for a gruelling game.

The hardcore of the Plate that have turned up are very keen to play and so are their guys. We wait for a break in the downpour and inspect the pitch. It is remarkably playable, obviously it is that sort of rain that has been falling this summer, the sort that doesn't replenish the supplies and means that hosepipe bans are imposed in the middle of a seeming monsoon. Unfortunately, it is the sort of rain that washes away pitch markings, so they are not at all clear. Apparently one of the ground staff came pout this morning to remark it but they did the rugby pitch by mistake instead. We are also going to have to put up with one of their guys refereeing too as they couldn't organise one and the league have yet again let us down. In the dressing room, the old problem of moaning before the game starts is evident. The pitch, the ref, the weather, and the fact that we have the bare 11 with Craig turning up at some late-point all give us excuses to start losing the match yet again before we have left the changing rooms. As I mentioned it before the opening game, it is more obvious to me now how certain members of the team are quite damaging in this respect.

Within a few minutes of kick off, it becomes obvious what Northville consider a football game to be: Moan and gripe as much as you can and if there is a ball near you start swinging and sliding. The first 20 minutes or so are distinctly in our favour as Northville waste their energy on shouting at their own bloke who is refereeing. Louis hits the bar and the post and finally scores with a tap in. However, after that point Lee starts to bite at their 'tackling skills' and in particular because they are targeting our youngest player: Ned. Once Lee has got involved, the Northville lot stop shouting at each other and turn on the new common enemy: Plate. With some of our minds now fixed towards stopping our team getting involved in the crappy, off the ball stuff, no protection from the referee and a few nerves failing, we gradually lose control of the game.

It is clear that Louis prefers running at defenders and not playing the lone role up front with his back to goal. James B is not really a centre midfielder, Reg not a centre back and Jumpy is clearly not fit after his ankle injury. Too many changes and people out of position. As soon as we don't have clear heads fixed on the game we've had it. Mind you, so has the ref. At one point in the second half, with both teams now nagging away at him. He grabs his whistle and throws it at Reg , 'You effing do it then' he exclaims. Reg's face was an absolute picture of innocence and shock. Even so, we still do not crumble. Ned scores on his first start for the Plate but it turns out to be almost meaningless as we go down 3-2. As I watched him score, I thought he wasn't bothered and had missed, but he was just so nonchalant it was untrue.

To the Greenbank. No Tony, no food, not many Platers make it though so no matter. Most of the talk concerns: 'bottle', 'guts', 'fear', 'spirit', 'strength', and other such words which are vital in football but do not involve the talent of kicking a ball.
Shirt of Shame: Lee (Russell Brand-ish)
Man of the match: Ned (cool finish)

Today's match can be described as a 'conflict'. It got me to thinking about the conflict we have gotten ourselves involved in. Since the beginning of the season (3rd September to today), there has been, on the news, in Iraq, reported: seventeen suicide bombings – 132 dead. Four battles – four dead. Also, In Afghanistan: one plane crash – fourteen dead. Five suicide bombings – fifty-three dead. One landmine fatality. Two battles – 137 dead. Six military operations in the Lebanon. 200,000 dead in Sudan reported. An attack on the US embassy in Syria. A Fundamentalist shooting in Jordan killing a British tourist. Brewing conflicts over nuclear issues in Iraq and North Korea. The Iraq situation on its own concerns a great many but just think how anti-war the populace would be if we were being shown the actual figures of 120 Iraqis dying each day. That would be 4200 reported deaths to watch. Would there ever be wars again if we were made to watch all the deaths instead of the edited highlights?

Like most people, if it had been known that this war was primarily about changing the Iraqi leadership, and not about weapons of mass destruction, terrorism and imminent threat, one wouldn't have been supportive. Blimey, we are asking a nation to accept that their leader is worth killing and for us to occupy their land for an indefinite period and what do we have to show them? Bush and Blair. Leaders who are fully aware that by following their economic principles, up to 30,000 children die each year around the world from malnourishment and not having clean drinking water. Then there is the damage that they know they are wreaking on the climate. It is a wonder that we are not constantly at war with China, Russia et al if it were on the basis of leadership change; we hardly have a harmonious relationship. Are we now going to war with Mugabe in Zimbabwe? Or with the countless other leaders around the world who don't rule their lands in the same way as ours?

Sunday 8th October 2006

Avon Plate versus Mangotsfield Sunday

Frys GFA Minor Cup Round 1
Referee: G Miles (league appointed)

Team:

	Sherry		
Reg	Dave	Jerry	Daz
	Bolts		
Ga	Yos	Lee	Ned
	Dr		

Subs: Simon (for Yos 65mins)
Ali (for Ned 80 mins)
James B (for Ga 45 mins)

Mangotsfield are a well-known club in Bristol. Their top team is in the Southern League Premier. They have loan signings, play in the FA trophy and I presume the FA Cup proper. I presume this lot are something to do with them although on a much lower level of course (these are in the Bristol & Wessex League). They have plenty of players of the large and fit sort, I mean they are massive. It is going to be a proper game today for sure. To aid that, we have a league appointed referee (hooray, at last). He has brought with him, two youngsters who are studying to be refs at some academy or other. With these linesmen you are spoiling us. We also have plenty of players and look resplendent in our River Plate kit. The Frys pitch is in top class notch too. Game on.

The first few minutes see the Plate under intense pressure. Thanks to global warming and the amount of running I am having to do, I begin to boil and need to take off my under armour. Even with a ref and linesmen, the tackles are still flying in and players are picking up knocks all over the park. Dave is already under the impression that if he shouts and screams, that will somehow help us deal with it all. The referee is certainly not in agreement with him. The game gets a little bitty with loads of breaks in play for the ref to have a word with one player or another. I am personally welcomed into the game with a deliberate elbow in my chest. All we had done was have the temerity to win a corner. Somehow, we are staying with them. At times, I find that I have been running non-stop for a time and am absolutely knackered. I see their movement and how we are coping and think that when we next play someone of our own division we are going to do really well. It takes a 30-yard screamer to get them in front and a 25 yard free kick puts them 2-0 up at half time. Yos and I agree that if we are still in touching distance with 15 minutes to go, we still have a good chance because I am sure they will be wondering how they haven't killed us off. We have been very one-sided down the left so off goes Ga for James B. Not the change to put the wind up them, but you never know.

The second half is similar to the first in that the referee is working overtime to keep the fouls and mouth down. Yos is booked as skipper for not informing the referee of the half time substitution; Dave inevitably goes into the book plus two of their players. Yos eventually takes such a whack that he has to go off for Simon. Sherry is kicked in the head and lies there whilst Jerry clears a shot off the line. We are not starved of possession but are quite wasteful with the final ball until James B puts in a cross, another one too close to their very good 'keeper, hang on, its only gone in. 2-1 Mangotsfield. Big ten minutes for the Plate but a simple cross into our box catches the defence ball-watching (a very common problem with Plate), free header. 3-1 goddammit. The Mangotsfield good mood doesn't last long as Jerry scores a rare goal with a 25-yard free kick straight in, was in as soon as he hit it. Jumpy's starting position and dead-ball specialist role are now both under threat. Now Mangotsfield show the meaning of being arsey, but as they get more mardy, we get more into the game. A challenge in our box, a good tackle from Dave? 50: 50 but Dave has wound the ref up all game, so penalty. 4-2, game over. 'Good luck in the cup lads, thanks ref, here's £20'.

After the customary drink at Frys Club, we head to the Greenbank. The talk is of how we usually raise our game for big matches and then lose it against more equal foes. Incredibly, there is a welcome for the heroes. A massive vat of curry awaits us. Whatever happened to Pizza and sandwiches? All this posh stuff is all very well but if it means we have to rely on the landlord's presence to get anything then we'd rather have the regular, more mundane fare. Plus, we are footy team and not the Rotary Club. Still, if that is what he wants to do then ok, but he will have to suffer the texts and written messages from myself.

Shirt of Shame: Dave (ref abuse)
Man of the Match: Jerry (top drawer free kick)

Sunday 15th October 2006

Avon Plate versus South Bristol Wanderers

Frys Bristol & District Sunday League Division 4

Team:

Sherry

Reg Dave Jerry Daz

Bolts

James B Yos Lee Louis

Dr

Subs: Ned (for Louis)
Ali (for James B)
Jumpy (for Daz)
Ga (unused sub and dodgy linesman but still got two votes for man of the match)

Today should be an interesting game. We played SB Wanderers a few seasons ago and they dicked us. They then went up to the top division of the Bristol and District League and have since plummeted back down again. We are also on the plummet but we never reached the heights they did. So who will be in the worse shape? Both sides have only won one match each this season so far.

We are coming off the back of a good performance last week, and excellent training on Thursday. We had yet again drawn with Easton Cowboys at Monks Park (we continue to get the pitch free for October due to their administrative error that means that our 2 teams (22 players odd) are sharing half a pitch). This morning we had 15 fit players turn up on time, we had corner posts and flags borrowed form Jumpy's school, him being a teacher and all. We have the best referee in the league: Brendan Slade. We even have a former player (Fowg) and Sherry's missus (Jen) cheering us on from the sidelines. If we don't win this one then I shall start to panic.

The kick off goes to myself and I beat 2 players converging on me, square it to Daz who proceeds to boot it into touch. I think this moment set the tone for the rest of the game. We would do quite well with the ball for 3 or 4 passes and then we would do something absolutely awful and lose possession. Panic, whinging, ball watching, oh you name it, we were doing it all and with little reason. Dave was doing his usual going nuts, at one point he was still shouting, but his mouth must have been very dry and his emotions running so high, that he wasn't using the English language any more. SB weren't that bloomin' fabulous. Somehow, these lads were pouring through us in the middle and the flanks. They were also taking their chances very well. We were creating chances because, despite our woeful use of the ball, we had so much of it that we had to have some chances. Scuffed shots, passes instead of attempts at goal, and so many crosses that hit the rear of their goal frame were our offering. One good reason for a bit of a stirring of Plate towards the end was because their no.10 (who had scored two of their goals) clashed heads with their non-running-but-amazing-at-heading no.8. The no.10 came off worse with blood, vomit and wooziness abounding. About 10 minutes later an ambulance arrived to take him away. I was near one of their no.8s headers and I had to move my head out of the way as it fizzed by. I could tell how hard his head must be. They then substituted another of their good players for a definitely not so good one. I even had a half chance right at the end of the game when I ran right through the middle and was about to get on the end of a cross from Ali. As I lunged for the shot I started to get a cramp in my right calf muscle and couldn't get any power into the effort. My other real moment of mention was a through ball that I slid through to Yos, but he scuffed his effort I am afraid. Ever since we started to play 5-a-sides together and used to set up lovely, intricate moves and goals, I have wanted to recreate it on Sunday mornings. This season is the first chance that we have played in the same team and in the right positions. It is definitely coming though. It will take one hell of a shift from us all to get back on track. This offering was not good enough for the gods of football and we ended up losing 4-0. I am starting to panic.

To the Greenbank. No Tony and no food. I felt we were too shocking a team to deserve food anyway so I didn't press anything.
Shirt of Shame: Jerry – forgot his boots, an honourable mention for Daz who had enquired of Jerry, as we warmed up, 'How did you get a short sleeve shirt?' the reply was Jerry motioning just how he had rolled up his sleeves in a cunning fashion statement.
Man of the match: Sherry – good distribution and saves.

As the laughter died down and Jerry donned the Rod Stewart tour T-shirt, Yos gathered up a load of coins and we all went over to the pool table to look at formations. The decision had been reached that we lost because we didn't have a common game plan across the team. The instructions had been for the full backs to push onto their wide man wherever they may be, the 3 of us midfielders would then put pressure on the ball and we would see how the other team fared. We ended up with a back four in a straight line which was sometimes nowhere near where their wide midfielders were, consequently, SB always had easy out balls to their width and then would be able to pass their way around us no matter what the centre could do. As different team members took their turn with the coins and discussed their idea of what we had been meant to play today, it was glaringly obvious that we are playing as 11 individuals and not as a team. No wonder we had been beaten. The only ray of hope therefore, is that we now have a common idea of what way we are trying to play, we are capable of putting it into action, and results once again may start going our way. That done, I proceeded to get absolutely wasted with Louis, Ned and Reg in the pub 'garden'. Then onto a table tennis league in which I reined supreme and I even managed to beat a non-Plater challenger in a couple of games as I was beginning to really spin out.

What a hero for the older blokes I am. Disappointingly for you readers, but good for me, is that by now, I am usually riddled with aches and pains of various sorts. At the moment, touch wood, I am hardly hurting at all. Of course, my knees do feel old. Other than that long-standing stuff, my left elbow that I jarred pre-season still gives me a bit of jip when I bang it. My chest is still a bit sore from where I was elbowed versus Mangotsfield. Nothing of note though. Does this mean I am luckier than usual? Fitter than usual? Not running around as much as usual? I can only try not to let it be the latter and I go into each game with the intention of being the best player.

We certainly add weight to the saying: 'Opposites attract'. Obviously, that cannot mean we attract partners because we don't like them (although at times it may seem that way), but rather earthy-types attract airy-types. Fiery-types attract watery-types. To compliment each other. To anchor the flighty, calm the raging, be whole and grow and progress. Without being actually married and with children, I really don't think I would have stuck at this lifelong-partnership-commitment thing. It is too easy to move on, make something happen to end it, get out of your head and, amazingly, things will go to pot. Plenty more fish in the sea. The wife is very special though so I am over the moon that we are getting the chance to have a real go at what could be a lifelong adventure.

Training this week was pretty good. We had 10 turn up so a 5-a-side on a half pitch at Monks Park. Two of the bloke were newcomers: Sam, friend of Sherry's from south Africa, and Pete, a 6′5″ academic friend of Yos who is apparently a good 'keeper and looked good at holding the ball up at the front. This means we now have potentially a squad of 23 players. I have knocked one off the total because Lewis has failed to communicate or turn up yet this season. With players not getting a game most weeks I don't think we can handle any more players.

Sunday 22nd October 2006

Luckwell versus Avon Plate

Hengrove Athletic Club, Whitchurch
Bristol & District Sunday League Division 4
Ref: M. Popel (League appointed)

Team:

Sherry
Reg Dave Jerry Ga
Ali Bolts Ned Tony
Louis

Subs; None

Alarm bells begin to ring on Saturday night. Yos pulls out with a 'bad cold'. Jumpy's ankle has flared up again plus he has been getting pissed all weekend because it was his birthday. I think he is trying to tell everyone he is 36. Oh, to be that age again etc. Simon won't make it due to the early cup kick-off time. No word from Craig but assume he is working. Korahn still can't do Sundays due to work. Lee is working (police shift). Daz is in Nottingham for his mum's birthday. Dan is still not doing the Plate thang for some reason. James B is away. Sam isn't available this weekend, cannot say why as he is softly spoken and has a strong accent. Other new-boy Pete is just coming back from an injury so won't be ready for a few weeks. Upon arrival at Hengrove we have 10 players. A 'phone call to the Dr reveals he has not set his alarm. It also transpires that Jumpy was supposed to be giving him a lift but another calls reveals he is only just about to get out of bed. Jumpy then has to drive across town, pick up the Dr and get to Hengrove, another six miles or so. These calls are taking place at 9.51am, kick off due at 10am. I tell you this, there is no moaning from our team, we seem to have no hope so we set ourselves up to have a game without playing with fear. We've only got to hold out until Dr arrives for the eleventh player and Jumpy can run the line. Fortunately, the referee is late and so we are able to stall the kick off for 20 minutes or so. We have to kick off with the ten men though. The opposition are in division 3 of our league after having been relegated from division 2 last season. So they are not going to be mugs for certain. They have plenty of players and one of their guys will run our line. The late-arriving referee assures us that the bloke is honest.

The first few minutes we are, remarkably, not being overrun. Dave and one of the Luckwell boys battle for the ball on our by-line. Dave intimates that the ball has gone out of play but their bloke carries on and gets in a Sherry-snaffled cross. Dave says something to the ref. Next thing we know, he's off! Lawks, we are now down to 9 men. Soon after, they get a free kick and I head it. The ball goes up and up, looping backwards. As I get off the floor, I mutter, 'Well at least it can't be an own goal'. However, the ball starts dropping rapidly, over Sherry's outstretched hands, and in. As Alan Hansen would say, 'unbelievable'. Within a minute, Ned decides to have a long-range pot shot. I look at it and I think it's strange, the net seems to be bulging as if it has gone in, it has, 1-1.

The Dr arrives. We are back to ten men. Jerry shifts things round so Reg goes centre-back, myself at right back, Ned and Louis in centre-mid, Dr up front. The rest are, of course, unchanged. My aim now, is to show how a fullback can push onto their winger. Thus, freeing up the centre-mid to be more attacking. With Ga doing the same on the other side, and the energy of the young 'uns in the middle we are playing some lovely football. Their extra man is in midfield and he has several long shots in the game. Unfortunately for us, most of them are wonder-shots that fly into our net. We reply through a lovely smack from the Dr, put through after some tigerish tackling by Ali. On the hour we are 6-2 down. From then on, we really turn it on. With nothing to lose, and the commitment generated by having ten men, we play flowing football. We draw fouls and their shape goes to pieces. When we can switch the ball (to me or Ga), we have acres of space. We earn a soft penalty for which nobody can actually see why, but we'll have it. I run to grab the ball but one of their players kicks it away so I miss my chance to take the penalty. As a nice gesture, Jerry lets Sherry take the penalty. It is low, it is hard, it is to the 'keepers right, it is to the right of the post. Shame, would have been his first ever Plate goal. A couple of minutes later still, there is a scramble in their box, it falls to Ali a few yards out in front of goal, over! Well, we could have been right back in it but now it's all over for our cup run, such as it was. Still, the game is really open and exciting. I am playing as a right-sided midfielder really. They score a fantastic header from nothing but we are creating opportunities and Dave and Jumpy on the sidelines are having a great time. With a minute left I receive the ball on the right, in their half, in space. Ned goes down in the centre-circle with cramp so the game is stopped. It resumes with their player giving Ali the ball who immediately passes back to me, still in space on the right. I burn up the wing, a slight wiggle and beat their despairing fullback. I look up to Dr at the near post so cross it for him. Great header turns it onto the bar and rebounds to Louis for a tap in. Whistle blows.

Dave apologises to the referee. The ref comes to me and says he wont send in the red card (and thus earn us a fine and Dave a ban). However, he wants me to make him sweat a bit and not tell him straight away. We do have to tell him pretty quickly because he gets really arsey when he thinks I am not doing anything to get the fine written off. He wasn't going to come down the pub even. As he is new, and not used to us that much.

We put him out of his misery and didn't give him too much grief at the Greenbank.

I have started texting the pub landlord during the week. Just to remind him that we have a game and will be down after. He left me a lovely message that he would prepare a welcome. Meatballs, cous cous, and a tomato based sauce. It must be like at Norwich City, having Delia Smith as chairperson. We clapped the lady who cooked the food, so hopefully she got a loved feeling. Talking of good feelings, I took the children to Macdonalds the other day. An old lady tapped me on the shoulder and said, ' You are a lovely Dad, it is so lovely to see'. I was speechless for a while and then felt a warm glow. A few minutes later, my eldest shouted out at the top of his voice and I shouted for him to, 'Shut up', which I obviously hate to say, and shows I am an ordinary parent after all. Sometimes, when you are just so knackered, or you haven't been out for ages, or you can't get space for you and your wife for any sort of while. When you work, see family, squeeze in as full a social-life as you can into an evening and a day. At these times you do feel a hero and it is great to hear it from someone else.

So many shirt of shame moments and so many good passages of play. The voting is very difficult today.
Shirt of Shame: Dave (mouth) Honourable mentions to Dr for his lateness, Cris for his Churchillian speech followed by John Major-type action, and I didn't get any votes for my own goal.
Man of the Match: Bolts (worked hard, spirit, anything that didn't mention skill really).

Back to Sherry's house to watch Man U (supported by Jumpy) play Liverpool (supported by Sherry and Yos who managed to drag himself off his sick-bed). Me, Ga and Louis as neutrals more interested in the joints being manufactured at a premiership quality pace. The televised game did not live up to this morning's fare, although Man Utd were excellent, Liverpool were trousers. I manage to go shopping for an ounce from a very lovely man and finally home for a calm and thankfully, eventually, an amorous evening.

This week saw the British army in Afghanistan start to hand control back of towns that have seen a large amount of violence. The local militias left in control are led and armed by the Taliban. Reports of 'American spies' being killed are in the press. It would be understandable that we are getting the heck out of Iraqi hotspots, but in Afghanistan we are just giving control back to those we are supposed to be opposed to in the ' War On Terrorism'. There must be so much information on Al Queeda, so many of its leaders, so many training camps. Get out of Iraq which has nothing whatsoever to do with terrorism and stick to your guns in Afghanistan.

Back to the real world. Can it only be a week since I was commenting on the massive Avon Plate squad? Only ten for the match on Sunday, now only nine for training. That may be an absolutely rubbish amount of players. The majority of those that were there decided to sulk. Apart from myself and the young 'uns, nobody ran around and there was a lot of crap footy played. Yos, Ga, Daz and Jumpy had let it be known they wouldn't be there, but the rest? Korahn has been in touch saying he is coming back to playing. A guy called Tyler, another young 'un has expressed a desire to return. There is yet another young 'un who wants to join us and he is a defender. Newly signed up Sam wasn't there tonight, nor was Yos' mate: Pete (presumably because Yos was away). Where Reg was I don't know. The Dr had only had a couple of days to sort out an alternative lift to the one usually given by Daz, one can't expect miracles.

Still, managed to have a pint down the pub and got a computer disk with the Bristol Beer factory logo, plus £100 for the printing. The landlord doesn't want to shell out any more money even though I have told him that the kit cost so much that what he had given to me was not enough to cover the kit and the Greenbank logo. Should all look pretty classy with the

Plate badge plus the two sponsorship logos. Tony was quite pissed tonight and was promising incredible food after the New Year, when he gets a new kitchen. He also seemed quite understanding of the Plate needing a bit of time to get going this season. The Beer Company guy, who is a mate of Yos and Ga and have seen him around our scene for years, was also surprisingly pissed by the time I left, for someone who works in the industry he was out of it. Good advert for their beer for sure. Between his efforts, mine, and Tony the landlord, we reckon we can get a piece in the Evening Post when the new kit bloomin' well arrives. Friday, no kit still. I ring the company: Kitbag.com. They have 'just discovered' that Nike won't be sending them the kit until 10th November with me receiving it about the 17th. The Beer Company need their disk back soon so I will have to get Yos or Daz on the case to get the damn thing copied. I sent a stern email to Kitbag saying how rude it was not to tell me for a whole month that there was going to be a delay. Will they knock anything off the price? Will they let Nike know how rubbish the service is? This is just another of the modern, shoddy customer services in British companies nowadays.

Customer service these days sucks. There is no debate allowed on this matter. In my job, I deal with the customer services departments of council tax, housing benefit, jobcentres, council housing offices, utilities providers, financial institutions, debt agencies and so on. All of them, bar none, are woeful at best. The usual is that you will have someone on the end of the line that agrees with everything you say, agrees to organise exactly what you need. A couple of weeks later, there is no sign of what you need and the company will have no record of the call and, in fact, could never have agreed to what they said they would do in the first place. Other common occurrences are the 'My screen has gone down', 'There are no advisors available, please call back', 'your call is important to us'.... So important they will make you wait for ages, speak to robots, make dozens of choices before... cutting you off. Or, of course there is the famous ' Please call back between the hours of...'

and it is between the hours of… anyway. Is this all a cunning ploy to put off those who have 'Pay As You Go mobiles which will have run out of credit before you can reach the desired human contact. With this marvellous computer age, we can now email our grievances and desires for information, this will prompt the 'auto response' which informs one that this time it will be a computer that will help to ignore you. Also, you will no doubt have dealt with customer services that are not based in this country, my experience of which is to immediately change the provider of that service because the person at the end of the line will be very hard to understand, they will certainly affect that they cannot understand you, will give garbled figures and information, and expect you to remain a customer, no way. My experience with an Indian one made me change from banking with Abbey national after about 15 years with them. They kept on about a large sum of money (about £200k if I remember rightly) they were going to take out my account. I hadn't a clue what they were on about and they scared me into quitting the bank. That, and the Abbey's habit of closing branches, thus making you rely more on cruddy customer services, was enough to see this loyal customer off. As a weird twist of fate, I now bank with a company that does all their work over the telephone and Internet. Because they actually seem to give a damn, and their business is utterly dependent on the 'phone and good customer services, they tend to get it right: not much time to get to a person, all the information is to hand, when something is said to be actioned, it is actioned. Simple really I love it when they say 'we may tape this call for quality and training purposes', what a joke. If they do tape them, it is only to listen to us poor sods trying to get a service 'against all odds'. If they are using them for training purposes, it must be for the 'Some of our clients are still getting through, how can we stop this?' training. With the masses of competition out there, you'd think the vast majority of companies would put in an effort, but instead they have gone down the route of one bad, all bad so what's the difference?

It does all add to the sport of cold-caller baiting. Here, you can either be as rude as you like to a telephone salesperson, or you can lead them on, being enthusiastic about their mobile phone upgrade, loan / mortgage, insurance, health cover or whatever, and then declining at the last second, as they feel they are closing the deal and counting the money. Thinking that it makes their awful job worthwhile. I was a tele-sales person for a couple of years, to businesses though so not quite so intrusive into people's lives and leisure time. Now, when I hear an introduction, a fact-find, a sales pitch, or a closing, I recognise the tricks they are trying to pull which is a great advantage and makes the game even more fun.

Sunday 29th October 2006

Portcullis versus Avon Plate

Yate outdoor Sports complex
Bristol & District Sunday League Division 4
Match Postponed: Pitch unplayable due to weather

Today is a beautiful day. Sunny, not much wind. Just enough of a chill in the air to promote lots of running around. Unfortunately, yesterday was an absolute pig of a day. It rained all day and at 5.15pm the dreaded call came to call it off. Shame as we would have had a league appointed referee. However, could also have been our saviour. This week, the communication between the team has been rubbish. I have done extra texts and emails but still, as of yesterday, we still only had nine players definitely confirmed. I am sure a couple more would have shown up, but I thought that last week. Quite often, last season, we found ourselves playing every week with a small squad and losing most games. When we had the call yesterday, we would usually have switched the game to the Bush and played, even though at that point we had nowhere near enough confirmed players. I try and get every game played because I need my Sunday release so much, plus, I don't want the season to drag on past march as it then impinges on the cricket season. Still, the Plate get a chance to sort out this communication problem, eventually my messages were f*** this and f*** that and sarcasm was used liberally and I tried to get across that I would actually like a life as well as organising all of theirs. Did not make much difference though. This day off also gives us the chance to, hopefully, have a decent training session on Thursday after last week's poor show.

Having this extra time, gives me the not-wished-for-chance of thinking about my relationship with my wife. She has been going through a rough time. Bringing up three kids (especially Louis who is in a very needy 'Terrible Two' stage relationship with her and demands a hell of a lot of her attention), means that she always seems at the end of her tether and miserable. Trouble is, she sees my 'escapes' i.e. marijuana, and she is resentful of that. If she smells it in the house at all, or sees the paraphernalia, she is getting more and more arsey about it. I don't mind the strength it takes to keep a marriage going. Inevitably there will be compromises and arguments, and the letting off of steam to those closest to you.

Added to this mixture is that I know I place too much emphasis on the physical / earthy pleasures and actions to reconfirm that things are going well. This is exacerbated at the moment because with all the cricket, golf, footy and the lifting that comes with three young children, I feel quite fit and sexy (this is quite rare really). The only thing to spoil this vision of loveliness is that I am, apparently, grinding my teeth at night a lot. Add this, to Louis sleeping most nights in our marital bed, well, there isn't much opportunity / strength for conjugals. There is my tendency to 'forget' when things are going on for the wife and just think her and I are not getting on. It doesn't help that my work seems to suck all the empathy and energy out of me at times and leads my other half to believe that I am the last one she could take her problems to. Also, that she has to accept that I am not the intensly-spirtual being that she must have wanted, just as she is not the sport-loving, dope-smoking, TV-watching, irreverent, sex-addict that I seem to want in the brief moments when I am single (I never end up with this sort in relationships though, and if it did, it would surely only last a short time, about the same amount of time that we have a 'honeymoon period' in any coming-together). So, there you have it with my thoughts on the matter for today. Are all long-term relationships and marriages like this? I guess it is the wrong period of history to be asking this question. Not many relationships last long enough to provide answers.

Whilst we have a break in games we can catch up on the early season table for Plate's division:

Team	Played	Won	Drawn	Lost	For	Against	Goal difference	Points
Brislington 1987	7	6	1	0	42	7	+35	19
Warwick	5	5	0	0	28	4	+24	15
Oracle	6	4	0	2	19	7	+12	12
Northville	7	4	0	3	17	21	-4	12
Portcullis	4	2	1	1	11	8	+3	7
Farmhouse	5	2	0	3	9	11	-2	6
Sth Bristol	4	2	0	2	12	15	-3	6
Longreach	5	2	0	3	11	23	-12	6
Cutters Friday	7	2	0	5	11	25	-14	6
R & P	6	1	0	5	8	16	-8	3
Avon Plate	**5**	**1**	**0**	**4**	7	**22**	**-15**	**3**
Queens Head	5	1	0	4	6	22	-16	3

Pretty sombre reading for Plate fans. Only goal difference is keeping us off bottom spot, and we are out of the cups. I suppose the only consolation is that we have lost to three of the top four teams. I feel that we are really getting somewhere (pending how this short term blip with numbers goes) and now we have to play the teams around us and Oracle who we have already beaten in the Evening Post Cup Round 1. Play up Plate.

Wednesday is full-on fantasy league obsession day. I am in my 3rd season of competing in the Telegraph Fantasy League Football Competition. 1st season I was just rubbish, ran out transfers early (managers now has 30 transfers in a 40 week season), poor start, finished about 5,000th. Last season was much better. Poor start but gradually pulled myself up and finished top of the work super-league and just sneaked into the top 1,000 finishers overall. This year has been terribly difficult so far. I entered 4 teams because I love the game so much and there are several prizes to play for, so even if my teams have no chance to be the competition winner, I can still play for weekly, monthly and highest-mover cash prizes. There is also the work super league. A good part of the Telegraph game is that on the super league section, there is a message board for use in showing-off, playing mind-games and general slagging off. My top team this season started in 73,754th place after week one, it has now struggled up to 63,290th, the team is now looking quite settled and has only used 8 transfers in 11 weeks. My other team that I will keep playing as a usual season-long game started off in 226,775th and has worked its way up to 119,691th. It seems there are about 275,000 teams altogether in the game. We are also up against Alan Hansen who picks a team and also, this year, they are featuring a team picked by Richard Branson, My top teams are ahead of them both at the moment. I am a lowly 6th in our super-league though. My other Two teams are doing so crappily (209,273rd and 252,601th) that I began to look at the fixtures for the month of November and formulating plans for a go at the monthly prize, use a load of their transfers, which I've hardly used yet (5 and 4 so far), and go for the weekly prizes along the way. After several hashish-smoke-filled-hours, staring at the computer screen and looking at all the permutations, I still haven't completely decided which of the Two bottom teams will go for it this month but what I did decide was that I would buy a whole new team (£6) just geared up to start this month well and get the most out of the November fixtures. My major mistakes so far: starting off with too many Arsenal and Liverpool players who played extra Champions League qualifiers and thus, less Premiership games (Champions League not counted in this game, only Prem and FA Cup.), also buying Mascherano and Tevez at West Ham. At least it gives me some interest in the Premiership until Derby County deem it worthy to rejoin the Fat-Cats club.

Talking of the mighty Rams, we may as well have an update on them as well here. After last season with Phil 'who the hell are you' Brown as manager, with his 'keep a clean sheet above all else' rubbish. This season we are spoilt with a top-drawer seeming boss: Billy Davies, formerly of Preston North End. Enabling someone like Billy to take over was the new board of directors at Derby County. Somehow, they seem to have wiped millions off the debt, restructured the rest in our favour, started the process of reducing yearly losses, but at the same time have provided some quite serious funds for Billy to build a team. With transfer windows, we got caught out. We managed to get out of the club, those players who Billy did not think were fighting for the cause (including Inigo Idiakez and Tommy Smith) but ran out of time to bring some more quality in. he had managed to get Camara from Celtic, Leacock from Fulham, Oakley from Southampton, Bywater from West ham, Howard from Luton and Ryan Smith from Arsenal. It is a joy to see Derby buying players for actual money, even going to the million-mark for Howard. Buying players who are under 30. Buying players from higher-level clubs. What especially used to irk me was that we had to usually get ageing rubbish on loan, get them fit whilst they played crap and then return to their original teams to go on and have a great season, Stern John being a good case-in-point last season. The only players we have on loan at the moment are Arturo Lupoli from Arsenal who looks bloomin' marvellous and the best non-scoring-striker in the world: John Stead from Sunderland. We in turn have 3 or 4 of our young 'uns on loan to the likes of Bournemouth and Bradford. Thankfully, our Academy continues to issue forth some great talent. Huddlestone may have gone to Spurs but we now have Giles Barnes. Just turned pro but looks the part. Great skill and scored two cracking goals last night as we beat the might of Barnsley at Pride Park. We are now 9th and only 3 points off the play offs. It is certainly never boring being a Derby fan. We do not usually finish in mid table. Up and down to the top level every few years with relegation and play-off scraps in between.

Recent times, we only looked decent when George Burley was in charge, but, as is the way with Derby, we usually sack our good managers (Brian Clough included. It makes me weep to read 'Old Big 'Eads' autobiography because he states that if he and Peter Taylor hadn't left in the early Seventies, we would now be as big as Manchester United. The sad truth is, you have to believe him) With Derby, we seem to get the bad luck as to when we meet teams. This season we have played Sunderland in Roy Keane's first game in charge and we played Birmingham in the game where, had they lost, Steve Bruce would be sacked. The Blues have now won four games on the bounce. With Derby riding quite high it does at least mean that when I go training tomorrow I wont get too much grief off of Daz and Matty, the Easton Cowboy Forest fan.

I have really been nagging the team this week about not communicating with me and having poor turnouts at training and matches. Thankfully, this paid off with fifteen of us turning up at Monks Park this week. I was on the seven-man team which included the reappearance of the young 'un known as Korahn. Also was his half-brother, the young 'un known as Tyler. They were also on my team and consequently, we went on to hammer the Eight men. It was just a good session though, the squad seems large again and we have a gaggle of young 'uns who seem up for it. In the pub after, I brought up the idea that if we lost again, we should look at the manager situation as his no-shows on Thursdays is not good for team preparation, looking at the players, developing systems etc etc. Reg seemed up for it as he believes it is 'his turn' and Jumpy would also consider it, I think he wants to pick himself as he hates being on the bench. Also, we chatted about the personnel. Pity Ga, James B, Ali and fringe-players, but we are losing most games and we need to get some wins, as things are dire. Therefore, rather than being considerate, we should play our strongest team. This would mean including all the young 'uns, with Reg and Lee at fullback. I text Jer our thoughts.

Sunday 5th November 2006

Warwick versus Avon Plate

Fisher Road, Kingswood
Bristol & District Sunday League Division 4
Ref: Norman Willey (League appointed)

Team:

Sherry
Jumpy Simon Jerry Daz
Bolts
Korahn Yos Louis Ned
Dr

Subs: Ga (for Daz 85 mins)
James B (For Bolts 89 mins)

I wish we had someone filming that match today. The most unbelievable match I have ever played in. One of the most enjoyable too. One of those days that make you realise what it's all about. A morning that makes you love your team all over again. The memories from this day will be with me forever. Apart from the 30 spectators and players, nobody will really know what it was like. If this match had been shown on Sky, my goodness, Andy Gray et al would never have shut up about it.

Warwick have, of course, already trounced us 8-0 in the first, dreadful game of this season. Since then they have won all their matches, Fifteen out of Fifteen points. I receive the dreaded Sunday morning texts from Reg ('A load of work on') and Lee ('son is in hospital'). So, Daz and Jumpy are the full backs, the young 'uns are picked with Ga and James B on the bench. Because Reg didn't come, meant Ali didn't get a lift organised. I picked Ned up, we thought Korahn wasn't going to make it but he made a good effort as I was driving near his house so got him on board and instead of giving him a lateness roasting, we told him to give his retort on the pitch. Tony didn't make it, don't know why. Craig seems to have gone off the Plate radar. Dave was working, good really as we have Jerry and Simon for centre-back and I'm not sure how much I trust Dave's mouth if today gets tense.

We start off okay. The pitch is not flat and has loads of newly cut grass on it. There are two distinct types of game being played here: Plate passing on the floor and Warwick launching from their big centre backs up to their two good forwards. It is an even game until they have a speculative shot that nutmegs Sherry from 30 yards. Disaster? We aren't put off and equalize through the Dr. We then fall apart. Their defenders find their range and start pinging balls that go over my head and bounce around our centre backs. No matter how much running I am doing, we have gone to pot. I have a couple of lousy shots. We are playing with trepidation and 'Pitter-Patter football' is rife. I haven't a clue as to what I should be doing. They start their attacks too deep for me to try and break up, but their launched passes are going beyond me. We have no ideas on how to build anything much of our own. Half time comes non-too-soon for us and we are 4-1 down. It is not a dirty game, the ref has control. There is quite a bit of moaning when we actually bother to try and win a header, but they get loads of free kicks out of it and that, perhaps , breaks up their play enough for us to only be that far behind at the break.

Usually at half time I am trying to get my breath back, having a Red Bull, thinking about my own game, and cheering at the right times when Jerry is trying to gee everyone up. This time though, I was desperate to get some instructions on how we should be playing. At absolutely the wrong time, the full backs had no idea on how to play the pushing up game. They were standing miles off any men, using the midfield to mark the wingers, holding a line with the centre backs, and generally being totally dominated. I say at the wrong time, because Warwick are using long ball tactics straight down the middle so there is no need for wide defenders marking space, get their players backed up and we will have a chance with winning the second ball and have some space to attack into. As I say, I needed some direction badly. You could only imagine their team thinking they had put Eight past us last time, go for the Ten! I put a bit of pressure on Jerry as I had in the back of my mind that this was to be the loss that cost him his position. To his credit, he changed the formation and explained that we now had two up front (Ned and Dr) to hassle their centre backs and cut out their long balls. Myself and Yos would hold the middle, two best mates who love footy and love the Plate, in the engine room. Louis and Korahn to give us some width. Daz and Jumpy to bloomin' well push on and force their wide men back. Gamble on the best form of defence being to attack.

The Second half kicks off. One of their guys shouts about not needing 5 minutes to get going this half. Almost straight away, they cross the ball low into our box, I intercept, pass to Dr. He runs and passes it to Louis down the line, across their box and Korahn blasts it in. Start of the half and we are actually worrying them. Not for the first time, a young 'un who has scored, now proceeds to vomit. Luckily, he only needs a couple of minutes to recover and is back on. Suddenly, Yos and I are winning loads of headers (admittedly some are with noses and ears) but we are competing.

I feel free to roam and now can start getting close to their players when they are on the ball. This is the case all over the park and they don't like it. A ball down the right channel sets

Korahn on his merry way, dancing past a couple of challenges and planting the 3rd goal in. Chances start coming thick and fast. I have a shot that just goes over from the edge of the box, korahn hits the bar. The Warwick long balls, few and far between now, are going straight through to Cris. On about 55 minutes, Louis slides a ball through to the Dr, the 'keeper comes out to the edge of the box and the ball comes out to me about 40 yards out (this is no exaggeration, it was others who were saying it too) on my left foot. I could see the goalie was not in a great position so I lashed it first time. As soon as I hit it, I knew it was in. The ball bounced just as I connected so there was a lovely badoosh sound. I looked up and saw it whistling toward goal and gradually it assumed a missile-type trajectory that had only one net-busting destination. I was aware that we were now 4-4 so I went absolutely bananas. Jumping on anyone near me and screaming expletives. All thoughts of a staged goal celebration went out of the window. My second belter of the season and both with my, 'swinger'.

Warwick are now losing it with each other. They cannot believe it and cannot do a goddamn thing about it. I can literally feel a sensation flooding through me as one can sense that the tide has totally turned and the other team have absolutely had it. Most of the remainder of the match I am in a nervy-ecstatic condition. Another ball into their box and Dr wallops it into the corner. 5-4 to the Plate.

There is still only an hour gone and I begin to think we cannot hang on for the rest of the match. No worries though as we just continue to batter at their goal. Jumpy, actually now playing as a more advanced right-back, wins the ball on the edge of their box, is tackled, 'Penalty!', he shrieks but the ball has rolled to Korahn who shoots, gets a slight deflection and loops over the 'keeper. 6-4 to the Plate and a bit of daylight now. Ned gets in on the act with a lovely finish right into the bottom corner. 7-4.

Now it becomes clear just how knackering that 20-minute

period was since half time. We have been an adrenalin-fuelled rocket. The rest of the game we are still in absolute control and they only score another consolation with five minutes or so to go. If we are tired, then they are shot-to-pieces. One reason they dominated the first half could be that they shot-their-bolt but running around after their own long balls so much in that opening period. I get Jerry to use our substitutions in a professional manner and run down the clock for the last few minutes. One of those subbed was myself. I had done a diving header to clear some danger and I got cramps in both calf muscles and my left foot at the same time. I literally could not run another step. I just had time to light a fag, and the whistle blew. 7-5 to the Plate in the biggest turnaround in our history. Ever!

There was much rejoicing. Simon's partner and two kids had come to watch, along with Simon's mother-in-law. Cris' partner was there, so was Louis' dad and Joff had chosen this day to come and have a watch. They (and the subs) thoroughly enjoyed it. The league table wont look so awful. We now feel we can beat anyone. We are playing the bottom team next week. I scored a beauty. Everyone had answered the call. All week I can go on about this to everyone I meet. The pub landlord is happy. This week he provides some fabulous garlicky sausages that even a vegetarian eats.
Shirt of Shame: Sherry (nutmegged from 30 yards)
Man of the Match: Korahn (skills, goals, vomit, the lot)

The Easton Cowboys are also in because their pub: The Plough is shut for a couple of weeks for refurbishment. They are not in such a good mood as they have been beaten this morning, 4-0 by Lebeqs Tavern Reserves. Lebeqs is a pub in Easton that proclaims itself, 'The home of football' in Bristol. They have several teams, two in our league. Their top team is in the Premier division and usually win the title and/or one of the cups. I have written previously that reserve teams should be disbanded from our league if they already have a first team represented. With Lebeqs, as with the other bigger teams, you don't know whether their first teamers are playing or not. Whichever lot you end up playing, the majority of them are absolutely massive geezers. An incredibly mouthy, arrogant and combatative bunch backs them up on the sidelines. We have had the 'joy' of playing them once before, a few years ago in the cup. We were thrashed 10-1, there was absolutely no enjoyment to be had from the game, just a question of survival. We thought that with a big win behind them they may actually chill out a bit, but no. There was a right old rumpus coming from their changing room afterwards. One of their guys was claiming that he had about £800 stolen from his pocket. He actually got to the point of strip-searching his own team and then coming into our dressing room to accuse us. The evidence is that nothing has ever been stolen from a changing room that has anything to do with us, the match was at the Bush and we can see the entrance from the pitch so no one can waltz in and commit theft, also, this same guy had supposedly lost loads of money before, so why carry that amount again? Isn't it obvious that someone in their entourage knows the money is there and is having it away? I sat outside and skinned up a reefer when this arse emerged and he took one look and nicked my bag of weed to, 'make up for' his, 'theft'. Very bravely, I waited until another of our team was backing me up and went to this guy's car to tackle him about it. He got out of his car, and kept going up and up until he reached his full height of about 6'6". 'You can keep the weed, but just know that you are an arsehole' was the best we could manage and let him and his dozens of massive mates leave us. I once went to see them in the Evening Post cup final, which is played at the Memorial Ground (home to Bristol Rovers and Bristol Shoguns). Two things were brought home to me: Firstly, Plate have to toughen up as a team. Secondly, the cultural backgrounds of our two clubs are so different and thus misunderstandings of meaning and so on will occur which only make a competitive game of football that bit more intense. Just like in life really.

I have, of course, no issues with any creed of peoples of this world. We live in Bristol for goodness sake, but this Lebeqs crew, when they are near a football pitch, are just plain nuts and if they are happy that they achieve success but despised around the circuit, then fair enough. Plate are loved and respected without winning loads of trophies and that suits me fine although I would love to get promotion this season. The rest of the results today made that a little more likely to achieve as Queens Head Rangers beat Farmhouse (6th), R & P beat Oracle (3rd) and we have of course beaten another top team: Warwick (2nd). Incredibly, in a division of eleven teams, seven are now on six points. Derby County look like trying to make it a promotion double for me as they beat West Brom yesterday 2-1 at home. They mirrored our game in that they were apparently dreadful in the first half and amazing after the interval. Fantasy footy has not matched real-life footy though with my Chelsea and Arsenal players tasting defeat at the hands of Tottenham and West ham respectively. This cost all my teams big-style, especially as John Terry is in most of them and was sent off (-5 points). The new team I bought would have been pushing for a prize if it hadn't earned just three extra points for its four transfers used.

Training was immense this week. We had fifteen players in attendance including all the young 'uns, plus a new-boy: Sam (who looked alright, friend of Sherry's). We took on the Easton Cowboys in a 12-a-side game for the last half hour and we won 7-2. Considering again, the relative positions of the teams, that is a good score at any time. Unfortunately, again, there was no video of the goal I scored. I tackled one of their guys in our own half, knocked it through his legs and felt his kick on the back of my legs. That just made me angry and I heard one of their other guys calling him some choice names. So, I set off, beat one, swap feet and charge into the vacant midfield, then a quick shimmy and I am through. Having come all that way I was determined not to miss so I summoned every last reserve of energy and lashed it in to the corner. By the time I had run back into position I was having chest pains but feeling exhilarated.

Shame Yos and Jerry weren't there. My best mate deserved to witness that, and if the manager had seen it then I would never have had to worry about my position ever again. The Greenbank landlord rang me up several times for an unknown reason, I later discovered he had been out all day drinking with our other sponsor rep of the Bristol Beer Company.

As well as my incredible goal-week. There was also the small matter of the American Mid-term elections. One of the many things that amazed me was Bush saying that whatever happened, he was going to keep on going in Iraq and his version of the 'War on Terror'. Now here he is, discounting democracy and yet he is supposed to be fighting a war to promote Western-style democracy. Democracy comes from the word 'Demos' not 'Dumbass'. It was nice to hear repeats of the Donald Rumsfeld speech where he talks of, 'the things that they didn't know they didn't know, they now know they don't know'. It seems that scandals of sexual and financial natures have led to the Americans voting for the Democrats, as well as the Iraq issue. The middle class is rebelling because where there has been economic growth, they have missed out and where there is economic slump, they are hit the hardest. The religious power-groups are deserting the Republicans because of the sleaze and lack of 'moral' agenda. The results were that the Republicans lost control of the House of Representatives and the Senate (Democrats and Republicans tied on 49 seats but 2 independents said they would back the Democrats). When I studied American politics as part of my useful degree, it was all about the personalities of candidates and the intense smearing of characters that happens during US elections, apparently, this is the only hope for the Republicans in the next election, that policies go out of the window in exchange for personalities (spin and money), how sad is that?

Of course, Bush may have been given a 'Thumping', with Iraq high on the agenda, but the President is in charge of foreign policy and the whole situation is such a mess that any alternatives to maintaining a military force over there is too risky. Whilst I was looking into this matter, I came across the typically subtle US 'Project for the New American Strategy', apparently drawn up in 1997. Also typical of the US is the fact that this project has lasted a grand total of nine years before crumbling. Nine years in American terms is practically ancient history and so will probably be seen as a great success. As was stated in 2003 by the mighty Bush was that, 'Promoting democracy and freedom in the Middle East will be a massive and difficult undertaking, but it is worthy of America's effort and sacrifice'. First point to this statement is that it seems hard to believe that Bush actually said it, it sounds like a coherent sentence, but also, he forgets to build in to his plan that the rest of the world may actually be a bit pissed at the American hegemony is imposed in so bludgeoning and thoughtless a manner. Maybe the Allies should wait until Saddam is executed and then pull out of Iraq soon after. Once any threat of him returning and leading some to glory, whilst reaping revenge on the rest, is gone, the country will surely be ready to take up its own government. We now have, basically, two 'lame duck' leaders who want to go out in glory, with a place in history. They have their fingers on the button. Facing them, are the nations who want weapons, such as North Korea and Iraq, those nations that are 'misplacing' nukes, Russia/old Soviet Union territories for example. On the third hand we have the committed fundamentalists intent on seeing the West in ruins. When mankind finally emerges back into the sunlight, they will look back and say, 'How the hell did they let that situation arise?'

Some say that the universe is in balance. To match up the welter of good news this week, there was sadness. Simon revealed that he is going to miss the last four months of the season because of a move to Cornwall. By the time the wife and myself realise our dream of moving down there, my Bristol scene should have transferred down there nicely. With the debt and commitments we have, we shall be in Bristol for a while yet though.

Sunday 12th November 2006

Queens head Rangers versus Avon Plate

Canford Park, Bristol & District Sunday League Division 4
Ref: No league appointed referee

Team:

Sherry

Reg Dave Simon Daz

Jerry

Korahn Bolts Yos Ned

Dr

Subs: James B (for Korahn 70 mins)
Tyler (for Ned 75 mins)
Ali (for Yos 80 mins)

Approaching 10 O'clock and we are looking a bit ropey. None of the young 'uns have shown up yet. Jumpy has a bad cold and doesn't want to play but has to start getting changed. Ga is away. No Sam yet. Lee is doing some 'family stuff' and Dan is still absent. Just gone 10 O'clock and here are Tyler, Korahn and Ned and suddenly the football world seems rosy. Another chappy showing up was this guy Steve from Warwick. He had phoned to see if he could come and watch with a view to playing for us. Things weren't working out for him at Warwick, they have moved their training to a Wednesday and they seem to have a 'no train, no play' policy. After roughly 300 games with them, he needs to move on. Turns out that he is 52 years old and once our young 'uns arrived we had 15 fit players and so he would be doing well to make it into our starting eleven. You never know with the worst weather yet to come, and we usually need bodies at training.

We are not the only not-very-organised team. Five teams have turned up for two pitches. Double-bookings are a nightmare as you have made all that effort, there is no problems with the weather but you still can't play or get back the lie-in time (not that I have any of that anyway). In the other match, both teams are wearing Yellow and we have to bail them out with the loan of our away, Argentina kit. Almost certainly the best kit they have ever worn (and they ended up winning in it too, and they gave us a tenner for our troubles).

As the team sheet shows, things were changed around a little bit personnel-wise. I now find myself pushed on even further forward. I swear that by the time I am 60 I will be up front and looking world-class. There is a stroke of luck. We were about to kick off with one of their team having to referee, but the double-booked game had a ref and he showed up and wanted to do our game instead so a proper game, lovely. The pitch is not great, lumpy and bumpy and clinging grass. The weather is great though, no wind, dry and chilly but not freezing. On a personal note, I have run out of weed so no joints before the game which would normally mean I am hopefully 'on the ball' from the first whistle but my eldest has tonsillitis again and was up and down a lot last night and with him, Louis and the wife in my bed, I had to kip in Louis' bed. I couldn't go to bed until late, as I had not seen any football results today to make Match Of The Day more interesting.

It turns out that I have had a superb Saturday again for my fantasy league teams. Incredibly, Derby County won again, away from home this week versus Coventry. The last two seasons we have lost 6-1 and 6-2 up there, so another hoodoo is broken.

Jon Stead managed a goal too, which probably surprises himself as much as myself. Still, I don't feel rough or anything and last week we showed we can do it against the big boys in our division, can we carry that through to a game against bottom-of-the-shop Queens Head?

Kick off and although Plate aren't firing on all cylinders, we take a lead with a goal from the Dr within the first five minutes. It is a simple ball from midfield, turning their defence who are playing an, 'offside trap'. Their own bloke is running their line so Dr had to be on. Whatever, 'organisation' or 'game plan' they had, was on the point of collapse for most of the game. With the young legs up at the front supporting Dr, we had enough energy to harass them into mistakes and aimless long balls. Although Queens Head are a long ball team we don't bother to go 4-4-2 as myself and my midfield partners are actually taller than their centre midders (a rarity) so we are wining headers and if it goes over us, the defence are dealing with it or it is running through to Sherry in goal.

It does feel like we are playing twelve men at times as the referee blows for foul after foul against us. He even gives a handball against Dave when their guy heads it onto the arm he had behind himself. To his credit, we don't hear a peep out of Dave's notorious mouth all game and he still manages a solid display. However, a moment of weakness on our left invites a shot and they equalize. Importantly, we create chances straight away and don't let them get too many ideas of beating the mighty Plate. The ball is eventually squared to me on the edge of the box, their defender misses it, I chest it down, turn and miss-hit a shot that falls to Yos with his back to goal, swivel and goal! Back in the lead. Yos' first goal of the season and I have the joy of setting him up. On the half hour mark, Ned attempts a cross from our left and their keeper nicely gathers it and then falls into his own goal, the ball is clearly over the line and it is 3-1 to the Plate. Myself, Jerry and Yos are now working as a good triangle, swapping positions as one or the other goes on a forward run.

They manage one corner and Sherry is awake to palm it round the post. Reg is having a great time as a pushing-on-fullback. The guy he is marking has a cold and so is really struggling against the little tank that is Reg. We are very wasteful in front of goal and could easily be double the advantage we have as we hit half time.

No need to reorganise at half time. Only need to guard against complacency. Luckily, last week is still fresh in the mind and so we know that, given a chance, they could easily get back into this. Next goal is vital. Within ten minutes of the restart and the Dr has crashed home another and the vital goal is ours. Korahn finally gets on the score sheet after a hatful of chances. Dr completes his hat trick. 6-1 and the subs come on.

We are rampaging from all positions but the decisions for the final ball are letting us down and chances go begging. Dr is guilty of dwelling on the ball and then not putting people through who have made long runs from the back. Any bits and pieces that are falling to me are just not connecting right and there is no chance of a goal for me today. Simon takes a free kick that looks so poor that I turn to get back in position but there is a commotion and James B has apparently scored a great goal with his head. By this time I am pretty knackered and although the game is a lot of fun I am glad it is brought to an end. We must remember that this team are bottom, they had an even shorter midfield than us, and we had a full squad compared to their 12 including man-with-cold. However, we must also remember that they had won last week, were on the same points as us, and we are still settling down as a team and formation, and we didn't play our absolute best. Very enjoyable to be the 'dicking' team today after so many hidings in our time, really should have been more goals though. Yos was quite determined to knock the stuffing out of the opposition so that they don't look forward to playing us again.

The pub is a very happy place. The Easton Cowboys are down again as the Plough is still being refurbished. They managed to scrape a 13-1 victory over Novers Park (who are usually quite a strong team and have been in the Second Division for many years). The landlord provides wonderful roast chicken and apple sauce sandwiches that really hit the spot. I have slight soreness in my right knee as it turned over today as I went to play a ball into the channel and slipped on the dodgy pitch. It was only the usually quick crunch and the knee was back in place and raring to go. My left ankle is also one large red gash, how and when it got there, I have no idea. Other than that, I still feel stronger now than for years. My hopes were to be able to struggle through two more seasons or so but now I don't know, it may get a bit silly as an old man playing with the likes of the young 'uns (Ned is only 18 this week). There is much cheering and the usual clapping and hollering for players as they leave. Another week of telling all and sundry about our terrific team. It was tremendously close in the voting and somehow I managed to get a vote, but:
Shirt of Shame: Dr (Greedy Bastard)
Man of the Match: Dr (Hat-trick)

Oh woe is me. Thursday I came down with a bout of flu. No matter how I fought it off, I eventually had to give up. I even went in to work so that I could justifiably go to training. If I had the day off as I should, I may have recovered sufficiently to go training but I would have had to convince my wife that I could not be touched or asked to do anything all day, and then go off to footy.

Whilst having to lay in bed and watch television, I watched a very interesting program. It fired my philosophical nerve-endings into life. It was about an explorer-type-chappy. He was in Mongolia this week. There is bugger all there except nature and these few subsistence-level roaming tribes. Not a trapping of modern life in sight. The people were weather-beaten. They were so happy. In my view, this can only prove that it is desire that leads to unhappiness. You reach Nirvana when you learn how not to desire. In terms of making it relevant, I thought about this in terms of the problem of the youth in our country today. Ned says he didn't get into gangs and all that, because of his parents. He also has skating and college and football, and weed, and his human beat-boxing and quite possibly other talents and interests. It must also be taken into account that he and his family are very comfortable financially. Putting it simply therefore, all teenagers are bombarded with advertising. Their levels of desire are greatly heightened. Even if they get some of what they want, they are being taught that nothing is ever enough. The result is the angry reaction we get today. It is not only from a small minority either, so it is not the so-called teenage rebellion. Looking back over the last century or so of rampant industrialisation, the advertising bombardment has gotten increasingly rampant and each generation has been angrier at the society they are a part of. Is the modern capitalist world creating humans that are just never going to be happy?

Some good news was the training report from last night. I had had messages from Daz and Sherry that they weren't going to make it, with me not there either, I feared for the worst. Turns out they had fourteen players and had a young 'uns versus old 'uns game. Apparently, the young 'uns started well but were eventually ground down by the superior organisation and stamina of the experienced Platers. Also, Yos has bought Total War: Medieval 2, for his PC so roll on Thursdays when I am better.

If I feel unwell, then my Grandpa has managed to out-do me. Gramps is in Bournemouth hospital with a chest infection and is in isolation. I could only leave a couple of messages to say I had rung and was thinking of him. The nurse certainly didn't give any impression that it was at all serious. My aunt Pat, who had let me know in the first place, didn't think it was serious either. It is so weird to hear her voice. I used to see a fair amount of their family as I grew up but then nothing from 1980-odd to a couple of years ago at my Nan's funeral. I hadn't spoken to my Grandpa since January when I saw him, at that time he was complaining of itching and feeling pretty crappy. Ten months goes by so fast. I wrote the old boy a letter a week or so ago but I cannot imagine that there is a connection.

Sunday 19th November 2006

Avon Plate versus Portcullis

Fry's Club Bristol & District Sunday League Division 4
Referee: T Wren (League appointed)

Team:

Sherry

Jumpy Dave Simon Daz

Jerry

Korahn Bolts Reg Louis

Dr

Subs: Ned (for Jumpy 55 mins)
Tyler (for Louis 75 mins)
Ga (unused sub)
James B (unused sub)

Thankfully, I was able to get a good night's kip and saw off the worst of the flu in time for today's game. Yos is away and Lee's wife and child are ill so he cannot make it either. I am almost glad as we look like having a massive squad today. I pick up Ned, Tyler and Korahn and by the time we reach the changing rooms there is a whole squad of fourteen. Ga turns up to make it fifteen and one too many to be able to play today. Although I am in great form and am enjoying my football, which is showing in the way I am expressing myself these days, I still feel nervous about being selected for the starting eleven (it must be about three seasons since I was last a substitute starter). As you will see from the team sheet, I was picked. This week, Jerry is going to hold, I have Reg beside me (he is a defensive midfielder) and so I am expected now to be the most forward of the three in the middle. Poor Ned doesn't make the starting line-up on his eighteenth birthday, James B has his partner and two children watching so will be eager to strut some stuff. I know Ga is getting a bit pissed at being on the sidelines. You wouldn't want to leave Tyler on the bench either. The referee is here, an old boy indeed. Lovely fella though and a referee is always welcome, I think it stops things getting as out-of-hand as we have seen when there has been no league ref (Marcliff, Lebeqs, HFB – Hartcliffe Fat Bastards, Lawrence Weston, Northville amongst the worst examples of degenerating games).

The pitch is superb (we still haven't won at our new home yet, see Arsenal and The Emirates Stadium for similar story). We have lost the toss and are playing into the very bright sun which will make heading difficult in the first period. However, after days of rain and cold and wind, we have a couple of hours in the sunshine, no wind, beautiful for football.

Portcullis are a great bunch of lads, play the game as it should be, hard but fair and enjoying the craic. Their style of football is more basic and route one. Their two forwards are very good though and seem to win most of the 50 / 50 balls. Cris is in great form and pulls off a couple of saves and although we eventually concede, it is only the one. Not bad with this sun glare, burning our retinas. On the other hand, we create chances galore and loads of near-thing-situations. Personally, I am finding it hard to get into the game. I am trying to play from box to box to satisfy my natural drive to protect the back four, whilst also trying to be 'in the hole' a la Rooney. The result is that I am getting stuck in between the play and getting knackered at the same time. Plate passing is not brilliant but it is enough to send Louis, Korahn and Dr away on several occasions and the wrong decision or poor finish leaves us very frustrated as we troop off for half time.

No changes at half time. We discuss going to 4-4-2, but stick with what we are doing for '5 minutes'. I had been extremely nervous before the game. In my mind, Portcullis were going to be really good and we would come down to Earth with a bump. Now, we could see that they were eminently beatable, but we were actually losing 1-0. Next goal is vital and all that.

Ten minutes into the half and the goal comes. For Plate fans the goal has goal in entirely the wrong end and it is now 2-0 to Portcullis. I am getting wound up but some of our players looking like they don't know what their doing in their position, have forgotten what formation we are supposed to be playing, are frightened of the ball and opposition players and have mislaid their ability to kick the ball where you mean it to go. Finally, on 55 minutes Jerry starts to ring the changes. A disappointed Jumpy goes off for Ned. Ned goes to right side midfield, Korahn up front with Dr, me at 'pushing-on' fullback. Now, I know it is quite an alien concept, but the way we keep asking our full backs to play is to 'push-up'. Push on to their wingers, don't call midfield back to mark this man. Ideally, push their player back into his own half as they have to worry about our play and not on building their own play. Jumpy and Daz keep saying they will play it. During the match you see them, standing 20 yards off the opposition wide-man, and calling the midfield to mark the man whilst they stand as sweeper-full backs. So, I want to show how I see it being played. Within a minute or so of the change round, Jerry takes a free-kick, goalkeeper fumbles it, I am in their and react first, to Dr and in it goes, 2-1. 'That's pushing up' I rage. We start having a whale of a time on the right. I have Ned and Korahn forming triangles with me and we cut through them, Korahn crosses it and Louis is at the far post to make sure it crosses the line. 2-2, with our goals coming in the space of no more than a five minutes period.

Now, Tyler comes on and we look set. Instead of the mouth-watering Ned, myself and Korahn triangle on the right, we now have a rather delicious Korahn, myself and Tyler triangle. For some reason, the game now returns to its previous pattern. Portcullis with the very occasional chance that Cris deals with magnificently, and Plate with the vast majority of the ball and chances which go close but not close enough. Dave even manages to get the old ref to give him a yellow card with a bit of foul-mouthery. I am almost distraught inside as the whistle goes. As I traipse off, Lee from the sidelines says how well we played and I really snapped at him, 'We've just ruined the good work of the last couple of weeks, we were rubbish in front of goal', and that kind of whine. Lots of handshaking with Portcullis, it was a really clean game. It takes me a good half hour, plus joint of skunk, to begin to really calm down although the disappointment of not getting three points will not go away. Daz is all very, 'three games ago we would have taken seven points', but I can see it as nothing short of the end of any lingering hopes of the title and even promotion now seems a distant prospect. It does go to show that we aren't in much danger of finishing bottom any more, but that isn't the extent of my ambitions with this season's calibre of Plate.

With four young 'uns devouring a joint in the back of the motor, I head off to the Greenbank. Tony is there and points to a blackboard ' Game casserole, 3pm onwards, donations for Children In Need'. Fair enough although 3pm seems an awful long way off. Yos arrives back from his dad's birthday do. As we are all voting, he is given a piece of paper and told to get writing. He asks what shirt o' shame moments there were and Dave's mouth again gets the better of him by remarking how he had been yellow-carded, so Yos starts scribbling. It is quite close for the shirt vote, Jerry with a theatrical dive for a free kick, Reg falling over when about to shoot, but:
Shirt of Shame: Dave (mouthy again)
Man of the Match: Cris (great saves at great times) (Yos did give Dave his vote for 'honesty')

The pub today is marvellous. The barmaid is a thesaurus of barmaid language from the good old days. I am 'love', 'angel', darlin', 'sweetheart' and so on. Makes you feel welcome, and with a big smile on her face too. Not like the one with pink hair who looks at us like we are the very last people she wants to see inside this pub and just grunts. The atmosphere is pretty good as we seem to settle on the fact, 'we are on three game run without losing' mentality. My left ankle is an angry red colour and is very difficult to touch plus, I seem to have ricked my neck on the left-hand side. It also feels like I have a slight strain around my right knee muscles. I didn't feel it go over today though so I'm not overly concerned about that or any of my niggles. I can now also, re-allow the happy thoughts to return into my mind of the mighty Derby County, and their resurgence under Billy Davies. With their fourth win in a row, beating Luton Town 2-0 at their place, the Rams are now in a play off berth and doing even better than Avon Plate. Unfortunately, the last group of us troop out without a show from the 'Game Casserole'. There is hardly anyone left in the pub by this time, so I pity the Children In Need contribution although the Eastoners In Need will have food tonight.

Monday is time for another round with one of my bugbears: customer services. It is difficult enough not to shout and swear at these people when I am being paid to do it as part of my work, but when it interferes with my private life then I do get somewhat cross. As discussed earlier, I placed the order for the new Plate kit in September with Kitbag. Originally it looked like about six weeks as the kit had to made and then shipped from a Nike sweatshop somewhere. This time period passed and I contacted them again but my emails and phone messages were ignored. Eventually, they made a dreadful mistake and actually put my call through and this time they assured me that delivery would be to my door on 17th November 2006. 17th November duly came and went, 'phone messages and emails were ignored again. This morning I got through and was promised that the 'team wear' chappie would call back at 12 o'clock, 'as soon as he gets in'. I finish work at 4.15pm and still no call back so I ring them again. Usual choices made, robots spoken to, dreadful hold music listened to, wrong department spoken to and I am through. Guess what, as usual the kit is just about to be delivered. He will just ring his guy in Derby (come on you Rams) to double-check and will get back to me. I wait, I have things to do, including getting ready to go training and that means there is a good chance I shall see our sponsors tonight so I really could do with some updated information. Bloomin' choices, robots, hold music, and he's not at his desk, leave a message? Why not, I am a blinking idiot customer after all. Result, no call back and I have to hope that the new kit is actually delivered next week. Once I actually have it then I can do a very stern email of complaint but we need the kit first.

Thursdays have settled into a very good session in terms of numbers. Fifteen again tonight, makes for slightly uneven numbered sides but this usually does not matter. Tonight it does. I am on the short-handed side and we are blinkin' awful. As far as I am concerned, it all starts with Tony and Korahn on our right. They are playing the same position, Korahn is pissing about in our own half with 'pitter-patter' football, reminiscent of our early-season showings. Tony takes too many touches and doesn't seem to understand what tracking back means. Thus, we are always out of shape, giving the ball away in terrible areas and being simply played around because they always have the spare man plus their extra man. We get dicked even though we have myself, Yos, Dr and Korahn on one side. Of course, this is only training. There should be nothing hanging on the result. However, Yos is very open about being a sore loser and I have to agree with him. I especially didn't enjoy the feeling of being rubbish. Once the rot had set in, the whole of our team were then woeful. I could see the positions I was supposed to be in but just couldn't get there at the right time. We don't talk. We have little or no shape, just rubbish. It made me wonder how the heck we got through our first three or four seasons when we were really dreadful. We had little expectation then I suppose, lack of desire led to increased happiness. A great spirit was forged in those times and I wonder if I have forgotten it a little, in these times when we are actually looking like pushing for promotion. One thing the team needs to learn is that if I have been involved in a loss or a draw, there is no point speaking to me unless you desire a rant and rave about how utterly crap we are and how dare we think we are any good or special. Lee did it on Sunday and got a mouthful and after training I was spouting away in the changing room. My theme was that my hopes had been raised but thank you Plate for crushing them again so I may be able to enjoy my footy more. Whilst we were sorting out the teams for training, it turns out that several of us went up to Ga to say we needed a linesman, he was not best amused.

Good news in the pub. We have booked December 22nd for the Plate Xmas do. The musicians involved ('The White with Red Stripes') have practice organised. James B will be able to deejay and has access to mikes. Looks like being a cracking night.

Sunday 26th November 2006

Avon Plate versus Northville Athletic Reserves

Frys Club Bristol & District Sunday League Division 4

Match postponed. Northville have a game to play in one of the cup competitions. It should have been played last week, but was rained off. The rules state that the cup game must be rearranged played at the next opportunity. As a bonus, I had forgotten to inform Frys that the game was off, but I received a call from them to say that the game would have been off anyway as the pitches are waterlogged. The real shame of it is that we would have been playing the nastiest team in the league but with the referee secretary of the league. He would have kept it a football match and we would have definitely won it.

Even without a game, I managed to injure myself. I have gotten myself a slight groin strain. I don't really know how it happened. I was wearing heavy boots because I thought I was going to watch a footy match at the British Aerospace Welfare Association ground, which would have been muddy. Yesterday, I had the three lovely kiddy-winks to myself whilst the wife went to a production of a Faust play. Thus, I didn't feel bad about still having my day out from the family. The plan was to watch the Easton Cowboys, get to the pub, and go to Sherry's to watch Manchester United versus Chelsea. However, all amateur games were off. To Yos' and we played the new: 'Rome Total war' PC game for the next seven hours or so. I didn't get to Sherry's, his dog: Muttley, had died last night so I let him grieve. He had the dog a long time and she was very old but it is still a shock. I must have known of Muttley since Sherry joined the team, some five years ago. Anyway, I started to feel pain in my groin area when I got out of my car outside of Yos'. We were swapping seats to take it in turns on the old PC battles and I felt it every time we moved. Whether it was hurt whilst getting out of the car, walking with my heavy boots or some other, mysterious way, I don't recall. My ankle is not nearly as sore though. I am struggling to shake off the cough that arrived with the flu but has decided to hang around, without an invitation I'll have you know.

The monsoon type weather, as predicted by the Global Warming experts: dry, hot summers followed by mild but wet winters, did not disturb the professional game much, only one match was postponed. Derby County were therefore, able to continue their fantastic, amazing run of wins. Five on the bounce now. Fourth in the league and only three points off top. Billy Davies has turned Jon Stead into a scoring-striker. The newly put together team is gelling quite marvellously it seems. A great mixture of Academy players, young or at-their-peak aged players, a good balance, established stars not deemed to be trying by Billy, have gone. Hoodoos falling hither and yon: We had lost 6-1 and 6-2 at Coventry and won, we had a rubbish away record last year, this season we have the best, We hadn't beaten Leicester since 1991 at home, we beat them. Ipswich at home in midweek could really put the Rams amongst the pigeons. We had 29,000 odd in the crowd this week at home to Leicester. More than Bolton had at the Reebok for the visit of Arsenal, More than Charlton versus Everton, more than Fulham hosting Reading and at least 5,000 more than anyone else in our division. Derby have been on a downer for so long it seems, that it seems strange to remember what a massive club we are. With a good board of directors and good manager, and we seem to have both, we can make it to the Promised Land. Hopefully, when we get there, we will have learnt the lessons of last time in a financial sense at least. Apparently, the TV money from next season is much more massive than now. The board that have come in appear to be financial wizards. When they first took over, they somehow reduced the debt from around £35 million to about £8 million. Everything seems very 'open' at Derby County now, trust is returning, belief and confidence is flooding back. It feels as certain to succeed as when Lionel Pickering took on Jim Smith.

It is the last week of this month's 'Manager of the Month' prizes with the Telegraph's Fantasy League competition. The team that I bought in especially has done very well. Assou Ekotto set up a goal, Lennon scored, Berbatov scored one, set up two and won man of the match. Lampard set up Chelsea's goal. Rooney set up United's. Dyer was man of the match for Newcastle. Fabregas set up Arsenal's goal. Barry scored Villa's penalty. All in all, a chance of around 58 points. The team wasn't far off at least one of the £50 runners up prizes so fingers crossed for Wednesday. I would love to see my name in the paper this week. (Can you believe I missed out by just seven points – one goal more and £50 would have been mine. I will now plan for an FA Cup team to buy at beginning of 2007).

Talking of the premiership. This Sunday was billed as 'The Showdown': The franchise known as Manchester United versus 'The Wannabees' known as Chelsea (Peter Kenyon this week stated that Chelsea would be the biggest football club in the world by the year 2014). How can this match be '*The*' Showdown? Even if the title is between just these two clubs for the rest of the season, Chelsea still have to play Man Utd at Stamford Bridge, so this week's match could only have been called '*A* Showdown'. Lazy journalism again. A result of so much coverage, needing so many journalists that they seem to be scraping the barrel in television and the written –word media. In radio there is less of this, I think that because there are no pretty lights and whooshing sounds to distract oneself, you actually end up listening to the radio presenters, so they are forced to think about what they are saying. The newspapers, for a long time, have only been interested in sensationalism and forget the truth getting in the way.

At work, you can add these issues to the list of concerns that I am having to deal with: a part ownership home-buying scheme, football hooliganism, more drug use, child access for fathers, domestic violence, overpayments of benefits, legal proceedings against a supermarket chain (with regards a fall on a slippery surface), the breaking of probation rules, seeing someone into elderly-related services and bailiff visits.
Blimey, it is only when you put it down in writing that one can see how much is going on, and the amount of different moods I have to deal with and shrug off at the end of the working day.

Wednesday 29th November 2006 will always have the added significance in that it is the day that my Grandpa died, the last of my Grandparent generation. He was 92. It seems that his heart, lungs and kidney had had enough and failed. I called my auntie Pat earlier for an update and he was 'strong', and then got a call to say he had 'taken a turn for the worse' but that he could live for another couple of weeks. At this point I cleared my diary for tomorrow so that I could go down to Bournemouth hospital and say my goodbye. Finally, I received a call about a half hour later and he was dead. A mixture of feelings since: frustration that he couldn't hold on until tomorrow, guilt that I hadn't got to say goodbye and I keep thinking that the letter I wrote to him may have pushed him over the edge. In it I had written it would be difficult to visit at Christmas and asked him why he hadn't been in contact and I can't help but feel that it might have made him feel like chucking it all in. There is a sense of relief. He has been waiting to go ever since his wife (my Nan) died a couple of years ago.
Apparently, he had stopped reading or watching television and had little quality of life at the end.

There is a little trepidation, I have never been to a will-reading before, it feels like they are like they are on television programmes like Columbo and all that, there is always someone in the family who misses out on what they think they are due and a terrible row ensues. A while ago, my Grandpa said to me to get down to his as soon as I could, once he was dead, or there would be 'nothing left', I hope it doesn't turn out all messy. I wouldn't mind a couple of things to help remember him by but it feels ghoulish to want to go through his stuff, especially if there is any nonsense about arguing over who gets what. I think it will be fine. There is also the chance that I may have to spend some time in my father's company, as there will be money involved, I don't see how he will keep away. To me it will seem a bit rude, as all he seemed to do was to upset them, take money off them or be out of touch completely. A fair few demons may need to be faced. The funeral may be a bit weird. He has one sister left alive I think. A few bits and bobs of family that I only see at these sort of occasions, no friends that I can think of, just his son (possibly), daughter and grandchildren and those related to them. I do not think I would know what to say if I were asked to do so at the funeral.

I feel a bit fearful as my own mortality creeps up on me; all of my Grandparents are dead. For years I have been older than my mates, in the main, but been one of the few to have surviving Grandparents, but no longer. A branch of the family tree comes to an end.

He was a strange old boy. Always been very intolerant. He was anti-European. Anti-Labour party. He hated the way Britain had become 'swamped' by immigrants (especially of the Black variety I'm afraid). The Jewish people were disliked with a passion; he had fought a war against Hitler and then ended up agreeing with his most vicious policy. My Gramps was certainly one of those who harked back to 'The good old days'. I remember my father would always play Devil's Advocate to whatever position my Grandfather took and make him look silly because most of his arguments were based on a Black & White and not well thought out basis. However, every school holiday, my brother and myself were shipped to my Grandparent's house and we ended up spending more quality time with them than our actual parents. We couldn't really agree on much but we always knew how much we thought of each other. I hope that was the case when he passed on.

I have probably, never thought about him as much as I have recently. He always appeared gruff and aloof, but now I think he was shy. He was driven in many ways by my Nan, and I just think he allowed himself to be directed about. When she was gone, he didn't really have the social skills to be near to us as a family. Too late now to see it that way. I certainly didn't believe I would be thinking about him as much as I am. My brother is most worried that our father will turn up; he wants to go as soon as possible if he is there. I have been thinking about it. I know there is a lot of my father in me, I don't agree with his life but I can see where they have come from. Possibly, if he is at the funeral, or the reading of the will, he will be a picture of what I could have become. He has given me so many lessons of how not to live your young life and how not to be part of a family.

Derby's run of six wins in a row came to an end though away at West Brom. I feel low enough anyway. It makes it much more difficult to watch Match Of The Day 2 on Sundays because of Adrian Chiles who, like most celebrity football fans, try and make out that they are the longest-serving and most dedicated followers of their particular team, and not just doing it to make themselves have any sort of credibility with Alan Hansen and the like.

Thankfully, training this week was a lot better for us all and I felt especially good after last week's disgraceful showing. Passes that were putting the ball through the eye of a needle, shape, chat and a lot of sheer bloomin' talent on display. To top it all off, the new kit finally arrived. It is numbered correctly, 1-14. It does look quite spiffing. Only trouble now is getting the Avon Plate logo off Yos. I also tried to look at the Greenbank logo off the disk that Tony gave me but my compy was saying it couldn't show it. Hopefully, Yos can get me the Plate badge design and the printing company will be able to get the logo off the disk. I have a funny feeling that I will give them the kit and the logos, they wont be able to read them off the disk and it will take me bloomin' as long to get the logos on as it did to get the blinkin' kit in the first place.

Sunday 3rd December 2006

Avon Plate versus Farmhouse

Frys Club Bristol & District Sunday League Division 4

To top off my marvellous week, the Plate game is called off again due to the waterlogged pitches at Fry's. It wasn't even a particularly wet week. The monsoon of the previous week has left the ground all over Bristol in a sodden state. There were no games played in our division again this week.

As suspected, when I took the logos to the printers, the Greenbank logo could not be read. Bloomin' modern technology. A trip to Yos' and we managed to sort it with minimum fuss. Hoorah for modern technology. Why couldn't the bloomin' shop do it, they had a computer and they must surely have knowledge greater than ours of how to open a file? With my Grandpa's funeral on Thursday, it has cocked-up my flexible time this week. The logo place is a fair bit out of my way. Oh well, at least I have it priced up: Plate badge £2 - £3 per shirt plus £40 set-up charge as it will be embroidered; The Bristol Beer Company and the Greenbank logos will be printed and be £2-£3 per shirt but no set-up charge. So, between £124 and £166 for the lot, hopefully nearer the former figure as we are not a rich club at present.

It was in the logo shop, that I heard the cricket score from the last day of play at Adelaide. Makes you proud to be English. The selectors have said, 'There are going to be very few chances for wickets over there, so let's drop our best wicket keeper. We have lost an opener to stress, do we call up a replacement, specialist opener? No, let's make the number three do it.' Now, I am an opener myself of sorts, It is plain to see that a number three cannot do an opener's job. The selectors went on, ' Shall we play a real spinner, one who could even look half decent when compared to Warne, one who has taken loads of wickets and is exciting and passionate? No, we'll play a slow straight bowler who doesn't seem to exactly drive fear into Aussie hearts. Hey, why don't we also play that bowler, Anderson, he has a cracking record with bat and ball. There is the question of guts and balls. Listening on the radio, it seemed to me that the English batsmen had gone out on that day with the wrong attitude. Survival should not have been in their vocabulary at any point after day one. I crashed out about 3am with England on 79-5, completely pissed off that I had stayed up for that drivel.

As well as the logo saga, I am having to cram a week's work into four days. Also, I have a re-arranged Plate match to organise this weekend. The likelihood is that the pitches will still be waterlogged but the game is against Northville so I need to sort out a referee if possible. My usual day for contacting the other team is a Thursday evening, once the local rag has been published and we can double-check the fixtures and details. Then I text and email the team, then go training. As the funeral is on Thursday, I wont be able to do any of that. I am almost hoping that Frys cancel by then. Also, it has come to pass that my Grandpa has left me his car. It is an old man's car: a Rover. It is in great condition, well looked after, but the battery is flat because he couldn't use it much before he died. So I now have to arrange everything with that in mind. What is making it more difficult is that the wife said she would drive me down, hang out with the kids somewhere, and then we would get the car started and both drive home. However, last night, she decided that was too much hassle for her and the children. My brother would have to pick me up from the train station. He will be laden with three children's presents too which I will need to get to the Rover and pray it starts. James (my brother) can't stay for long after the funeral whereas I will be going to the food and drinks do in a pub, then back to Gramps old flat as he left instructions that I could pick up whatever I wanted. Blimey, it is a lot to think about. It is difficult enough, thinking about the funeral, let alone everything else going on this week. Perhaps I should mention that the missus was in a state last night, tired out, thinking she's a crap mum, worried about money. I tried to say the right things but my mind is in a bit of a whirl at the moment.

At the funeral were nine people in total, not bad considering he outlasted the vast majority of his family and friends. The wife drove me down in the end, with the children. I went to the burial. First time I have been to one of those. So we did all the sprinkling of soil into the seemingly very deep hole onto the casket, and could say goodbye. There was an Omen-type wind and the coffin-bearers were having to hold onto the ageing, female vicar. In the pub after, my cousin remarked that she thought the wind had come up because my Nan's ashes were being buried with my Grandpa and she wasn't happy about it. I can understand why people say that, it seemed he held her back in denying her any sort of social whirl but I hope they attracted each other because they were different. It does make you wonder though, what if you are married for sixty-four years and have to spend eternity together even though you weren't happy in the marriage. We got the car started no problem and it drove like a dream on the way back to Bristol. It was weird to go to his place after some food and drinks in a pub. He had left instructions that I could have what I wanted. Aunt Pat has been down several times since he died and so was used to it, but I was a little freaked out by it all. The wife arrived and we ended up with a carload of stuff. Pat wouldn't hear the word 'no' and that if we didn't have it, it would all go to charity. Pity we live a good three hour drive away, we didn't have time to go through his stuff and remember old times, just have a rummage around. After driving back, for three hours, in his old motor. I got in a bit of an emotional state and had a good cry. I wish that he and Nan were alive for one more year but they were both well. I just really hope they knew how I felt about them. I told them I loved them a fair amount once I was an adult, so that's good.

Sunday 10th December 2006

Avon Plate versus Longreach Athletic Reserves

Fry's Club Bristol & District Sunday League Division 4

Well, let us hope that I have a better week than the last couple. It starts off the same though with the game called off because of waterlogged pitches. We were supposed to play Longreach, then it was changed to Northville Athletic and finally, we had another match fixed up when the match was called off anyway.

It would be good to now shrug off the lethargy and depression since my Grandpa died and return to my usual self. I think that this will happen when I sell the Rover and put his stuff away. Christmas should perk me up as well. I miss the adrenalin rush of the footy too. My knees are beginning to hurt, my stomach is growing and it feels like we will need 'another' pre-season to get back in shape. Hopefully, we will have the advantage. We have so many of the young 'uns. They will stay fit and alert so if the rest of us can match other teams (and no-one else is playing at the moment either) then we should do okay. Only one more match possible before the yuletide break now anyway.

We certainly wont be playing any games this year with our new kit. I had a call in the week to say that the Plate crest logo I had given to the printers/embroiderers is too small. It is going to take a few days to get a new one together, take it up to the embroiderers, have them do the badge and get it back.

An incredible nineteen players at training this week. This figure includes another new guy, called Patrick. He is worth a special mention as he is a six-foot-plus man who can head the ball, is pretty good with the ball at his feet too, and can play centre back. With Simon going very soon this is the one position (other than 'keeper of course) where we don't have good cover. Training uncovered the mystery of my red and sore left ankle; my shin pads do not have any extra ankle support and so the one on my left leg slips down and rests, and rubs, on the ankle. It became clear as I pulled the shinny off after the session and there was blood and the mark, right where the shin pad had been. My right knee medial ligaments feel a bit sore. Also, I have developed a worrying left ankle pain. The sort of movement that sets it off is the action of pushing the clutch down on our motors. Some of the time there is a loud click and pain, sometimes just the pain and occasionally no pain or click. The lottery, whenever I put my foot down to change gear, is not exactly exciting as scary and groan inducing. The final pains I have noticed since training is that when I kneel down on my left knee, to turn on Christmas tree lights etc, there is a very sharp and distinct pain in the kneecap. When I was looking into knee injuries, when my cruciate had gone, I remember reading about 'housewife's knee' from scrubbing the outdoor step. Perhaps I have a version of that to add to my niggles. Certainly, I have nothing that would put me off playing and diving around, should the game actually be played. The team members who have been in touch with myself this week, including the young 'uns, are absolutely gagging for a game which is always a good sign.

Sunday 17th December 2006

Avon Plate versus Cutters Friday Reserves

Fry's Club Bristol & District Sunday league Division 4
Referee: J Passco (league appointed)

Team:

	Sherry	
Jumpy	Reg Jer	Daz
	Bolts	
James B	Yos	Louis
	Korahn	Dr

Subs: Lee (for Jumpy half time)
Ned (for James B half time)
Dave (for Louis 70 mins)
Ga (unused sub)
Ali (unused sub)

Naturally, as Plate are on an excellent run of results, Jerry announces that we are to play a new formation. A 4-1-4-2. I am again in the holding midfielder role but everything around me is changed. The words of wisdom in the pre-match team talk is that apparently 'everyone knows what to do so do it'. Unfortunately, that blatantly isn't the case. Individual groups gather to try and come up with a plan. For example, Yos, myself, Louis and James B get together and we stress the need to try and stay close together and work as a unit. The last thing we need, we state, is for me to end up twenty yards behind Yos who is twenty yards away from either Louis or James. Again, the full backs have different ideas to each other as to what 'pushing up' means. Korahn will have to play with his back to goal and thus will lose the obvious strength of his: running at defenders with his speed, energy and trickery. The opposition are a strange lot, considering they only have the same points as us. Not one of them is over mid-twenties in age and their body-fat count would be slightly below ours for sure. I sense this may not be their reserves at all. With hardly any games being played around Bristol today, Sunday first-teamers and Saturday players will be looking for any playing opportunity. Still, we have too many players to all get a game, the weather is perfect; a slight chill and hardly any wind, only the bright sun is a slight concern. We have a proper referee. The pitch is a bit sticky but the ball will zip around on the wet grass.

A few minutes into the game and our midfield engine has broken down. The cogs are spinning away but they are not connected together properly and no momentum is generated. Louis and James B are playing as orthodox wide men and Yos is way ahead of me. Exactly what we didn't want. Jumpy is ending up standing in no mans land and has no contact with James B either. The front two are witnessing our poor start and react by mistrusting the rest of the team. Consequently, there is very little linking up of our play from front to back. We are working our socks off and it must be a brilliant game for their supporters to watch as they obviously have the upper hand.

Because we don't know exactly what we should be doing, our communication is very poor. Countless times we are dispossessed when a simple 'man on' or offers from others to receive the ball would have kept us in possession. Soon, we cannot string any passes together at all. Inevitably their first goal comes. The game is about twenty minutes old when they score from a corner with a diving header. Reg holds his hands up as his man just waltzed off him to have a free header, fine one though it was. I have scored from diving headers before and they give you a hell of a feeling. We accept Reg's apology but feel it prudent to point out that he should concentrate on his own game as well as shouting at everyone else. He has a manful game at centre back but I don't know whether this is his best position. He ball-watches a tad too much and the opposition strikers find it too easy to spin away from him and grab that crucial couple of yards in and around our box. Cutters start to earn their own luck. They are pressing hard on us so that we are finding it increasingly difficult to build anything of our own and, because we are playing so far from each other, we win the odd tackle and header but the second ball keeps on falling to their feet. A classic example of this is on the half hour mark when they are awarded a free kick which is swung into our box, I win the header but it falls straight to their guy's feet and he puts it away. 0-2. With their confidence oozing, Cutters score a third, direct from a free kick some twenty yards out which flies straight in. 0-3 and half time at last.

Now the fun starts. The accusations are flying. There are about four different conversations going on. The frustrating thing for me is that when I try and chat about what is going on in certain positions, those players tend to take it as a personal insult. 'It wasn't me it was everyone else', is pretty much what is usually said. A favourite always seems to be to blame the midfield, 'not winning headers', 'big gap in the centre', 'not following their players', my goodness there are loads of them. We could have a rubbish goal kick go straight to their forward, with four defenders on him, he scores somehow, it therefore must be midfield's fault. When I was moved out of midfield due to my knee injury, I used to blame my replacements just the same, 'if you want to play in a glamour position you have to earn the right'. Jumpy starts to argue about how he is working the hardest and is the strongest player when Jerry 'jumps' in and subs him and James B, with Ned and Lee coming on. Daz is switched to right back and Lee goes in at left back, Ned on the right of midfield. It is worth noting at this point that Daz must have sliced four or five balls into our own box in the first half, so perhaps Jumpy is unlucky to come off but unfortunately for James B and himself, the right hand side has looked weak and most of our limited play has gone down the left. James B has got quite a lot of fouls into his time. The old problem of his: first movement too slow and when he reaches the ball he has opposition players ahead of him and so in he clatters.

Straight from the kick off we can sense this will be a good half for us. Within two minutes we have a great chance when the ball is crossed into their box but Yos screws his mid-air shot just wide. Cutters are a good team. Even though we are much improved they do not crumble and have enough talent to keep some possession going. The first twenty minutes of this half, they are under a good deal of pressure and we are rewarded with a lovely goal. Korahn plays the ball through for Louis who takes it in his stride, outpaces their defender and slots it home. 1-3. For the rest of the match it is a classic game of Plate trying to attack and Cutters catching us on the break. Jerry brings on Dave for the last quarter of an hour in place of a tiring Louis. Jerry can now throw himself up front to try and save the match. The whole match has been played in a 'hard but fair' manner, within five minutes of Dave coming on, he is shouting at the ref, pushing and shoving and arguing with their players. I try and remember that it is good for your centre back to be a no-nonsense, take no prisoners sort and I leave it to others to calm him down. Their 'keeper makes some tremendous saves, especially one where Ned was one-on-one with him and the 'keeper saved it. Guess who had charged up and was standing a few feet from Ned with an open goal in front of him? Me of course but you can't blame the lad for having a go. The final insult is a throw in to Cutters. Bouncy bouncy goes the ball as it slowly goes by our entire bloomin' defence and rolls gently to their guy to make the final score Avon Plate 1 Cutters Friday 4.

As usual, the first half hour after the match I am not worth speaking to, just babbling negative bollocks. At one point, we

had to stop the game so that the goal nets could be fastened properly. Also, we had been given the worst changing rooms, just a corridor with a couple of benches and a token clothes hook or two. This was even though there were only two matches being played, the Fry's guys just didn't want to have the bother of opening and cleaning the other changing rooms. We pay a heck of a lot for the privilege of playing here though so were feeling aggrieved. In protest, we did not have a drink in the Frys Club and went straight to the Greenbank. A few of us were keen to sit down and chat about what had gone wrong, without anyone feeling we were personally attacking them. I would love some pointers to get our midfield back working well, and don't pretend that I had anything like a good game today. Jumpy had his Dad's birthday to attend and a couple of others didn't make it to the pub. The man of the Match voting then distracted us.
Shirt of shame: Ned – missing a sitter when could have passed to Bolts
Man of the match: Reg – for being a strong man.

That was fun but Ga then cornered Jerry for some considerable time, Ga wanting to obtain an explanation as to why he wasn't being picked and played even though he kept turning up. Ga doesn't mind if Jerry doesn't think he is good enough, but would do something else with his Sunday mornings. Jerry then explaining the difficulties of being the Sunday morning manager. The choices between good mates, making substitutions in the heat of battle, not seeing us at training and so on. By the time he had finished with Ga, it didn't seem fair to chat more about the match. It is quite obvious that he is not enjoying that part of his Plate life and will be giving up the role at the end of the season. A bonus could be, he is returning to Thursday night training from the New Year. We will be able to chat/influence him more and he can see who is in form and there are newish players, such as Patrick and Tyler that he needs to watch in order to play them in their best position.

A couple of beers and joints later (no food though, some big do last night has left the management in a state) Louis challenges me to a table tennis match. None of my niggles gave me any grief today and there are no new injuries to report so I accept with glee. I end up thrashing him, Reg, Dr and Sherry a few times before I am too knackered to continue. There was no way I was going to lose at anything else today.

Tuesday this week is worth a mention as the mighty Plate saved it from gloom and despondency. Two cards had come through the door for me to collect stuff from the Post Office. One was a Christmas present for the wife. The other was a letter that I had to pay £1.23 postage charge for. It turned out to be from work and so I was immediately in a bad mood, having to pay for my own work post. Turns out that our government funding is renewed in March and they are worried because our service is deemed as 'expensive'. One way in which they want to address this is to reduce our wages. This put me in a much darker mood. I tried to get the petty cash back for the postage and there was noone around. Darker mood still. My pay packet is in my in-tray. No travel expenses are included (£90 odd). There is an email dated the 12th December from our manager saying he has 'just got a pile of forms, too late for this month's pay'. However, I have proof that they went up to him on the 5th, in plenty of time to meet this month's pay deadline with our finance department. Mood officially black. Personally, I would look at cutting out 'extraneous' parts of our service. If the government want to cut funding to mental health services then fine. However, don't expect us to then be able to introduce new ways of working and initiatives, to get the service users more involved, and for our staff to be trained to the highest level. You cannot pay less and not expect a decrease in service but as long as the front-line staff are protected and motivated, then at least the delivery of service face to face with the client will not suffer. Immediately, and not for the first time, I began to research the possibilities of Direct Payments in which the client sets up the type of support they need, get it agreed by a care-coordinator, and receive the funding from Social Services. They would then be employing me directly. As a large organisation, my work's charges would be vastly undercut but still give me the living I would deserve and the government would save money, and the client would be happy because they would still have me as their worker and I would be much more motivated as I would be working for myself.

It is incredibly annoying though, when you consider the £7Billion that has been spent on Iraq (959 attacks per day at present, plus the Gaza region is in turmoil once more). That money could have gone on goodness knows what, but a tiny part would sort out a quality service for those parts of society that are the detritus of a modern, ultra competitive, ultra consuming and transitory society. It galls me that there are increasing numbers of extremely wealthy people who would rather live behind massive steel gates, not be able to walk around alone at night, have alarms and cameras everywhere rather than spare a few dimes to build a community spirit and at least give the illusion that we are all in this crazy world together. We must remember that without street cleaners, high-fliers wouldn't be able to get to their offices because of all the rubbish and vomit etc. Then nobody would make any money. One shouldn't look down on the cleaner just because somebody somewhere has deemed that this should be so, they are integral. The 'sick and vulnerable' are an inevitable consequence of the way we live and work, the way that the awfulness of human nature and desire is bombarded at us all twenty four hours a day. So, don't look down on them, and think they do not deserve our generosity. For someone to be rich today, there are people who are picking up the pieces of shattered lives.

A letter for me, a large letter with 'Do not bend' on the brown envelope. It is a rather lovely certificate, which reads:

What a shot in the arm. I had a call from Jumpy within a minute of opening it and I gushed it all out to him before he could even say hello. An added bonus is that there is a blinkin' prize with the honour. A match ball from the sponsors based in Kingswood. That must be about £50 worth and if they have Puma ones then it will be a mighty prize indeed. This is either a new award or that we have just never won it before, however unlikely that seems.

The final piece of footy action for the Plate comes in this week's training. Fifteen hardy souls turn out in the fog for one of our better sessions, excellent passing, good shape and class finishing. My personal highlight of the evening was when Reg came hurtling after a ball which I had just cleared with my left. He came crashing through onto my right, standing foot; leg and his knee nestled not so gently onto mine. I looked down as, in slow motion, my knee and leg bent horribly out of shape under the weighty challenge. I thought, 'ooh, I'm going to have to pop that all back together now', however, I stamped my foot, ran a little, and it was okay. What a relief. If my knee can stand up to that, then it can stand up to most things that are going to be thrown at it on a Sunday morning. Proof conclusive. It will obviously be a little sore but let us hope it does not stop me dancing and leaping around tomorrow at the Avon Plate Christmas Do 2006.

DJ, Live Bands, Buffet, Drinking, Dancing Party type thing Ah...

The sound of a mass of drunken bodies singing the intricate harmonies of the old classic: 'Avon Plate are on the piss again', still rings around my head. A beautiful rendition without much rehearsal except for the last ten years occasional blast. Another unrehearsed moment came when I had had a few ales and I decided that, as I had never done it before, I would strum a guitar through an amplifier. There was a goodly amount of music apparatus around as the Avon Plate band: 'The Red and White Stripes' had played a fantastic gig (highlights 'The Avon Plate Blues' and 'Ring Of Fire') and DJ James B had also done a funky set. As I was messing about, Reg got on the drums, Dan got hold of the bass and Dr leapt for his lead guitar and we were off with an improved version of the Beatles' 'Paperback Writer'. A dream-come-true, to play live on stage in a band in front of people in a pub, fantastic. The wife had also come along for an extremely rare outing for the both of us to be together with a large number of my mates, nothing untoward happened and the missus had a lovely time, so another dream come true. The taxi even turned up on time so a great night all round

Ga [foreground] and Reg display the ecstasy of being involved with Avon Plate

It really happened! My live debut with axe.

James B couldn't be as good a footballer as a DJ or he would be in the Premiership and not the Sunday League

Is it really him? Yes, it is the long-lost Dan.

Sherry and Daz show how it shouldn't be done.

Lead scorer, lead guitarist, the Dr in full-flow, always a great sight.

Yos and Si show off the soon-to-be-replaced kit that has earned us the title of 'Prettiest Team in the League'

My knee had cleared up remarkably quickly so that didn't hold me back at all; unfortunately; somehow there has been the return of a mysterious and nasty shoulder complaint. It feels like my right shoulder blade has had all the cartilage and sinew removed. Thus, I have a dry joint, which grates around like someone has their elbow jammed into my shoulder. The pain and pins-and-needles, shoots down my arm and into my elbow. The pain is niggling but constant. It seems worse at night when I try to get to sleep, as I cannot find a painless position. I therefore, spin round and round until completely exhausted when I finally fall asleep. I usually become exhausted just when I am supposed to be waking up for the day. As mentioned earlier, I have had this injury before, about a year ago. At the time I spent a small fortune at the Sacro-cranial therapist and the problem was linked to a lack of communication with my wife, which led me to 'carry the weight of the world on my shoulders', thus a shoulder injury. This time I cannot say that is true, although if it is a stress-related injury then the kind letter from work in pre-Christmas week informing us of probable wage cuts, cannot have helped. This time around I cannot afford to get any private treatment, I can't think of an incident where my shoulder would have been damaged, and as it feels exactly the same as in the past, there must be some long-term damage in there for which I will need a scan and physio referral.

After a Christmas that was sadly disrupted by my pain and thus depression, we also struggled with my eldest and the wife coming down with Tonsillitis, and my daughter having an ear infection. I finally caught it on New Year's Eve. A couple of nights in a soaking wet bed from the sweats, occasional shivering bouts, no energy at all, no appetite, pain whenever one swallows or drinks, nose and throat full of goo, plus the shoulder is still making it impossible to find a sleeping position. I managed to sit and watch the wife and Louis dancing around as the midnight chimes went off. The missus is such a beautiful person inside and out, made me feel better for a moment. For certain, no matter how ill I was feeling, Saddam Hussein is in a slightly worse state as he was hung for his crimes against humanity. Now didn't Jesus say something in the region of, 'we should not judge lest we be judged ourselves'? If so, there are a few 'leaders' who should (but wont) be quaking in their boots.

It was turning out to be the usual case of the main difference between being a married person and a single one is that you very rarely become ill and have the chance to take care of yourself. There is either always something going on which one has to battle through, or there is always someone else in the family who is ill too and has to be looked after at your expense. Firstly, the rest of the immediate family all took ill at some point over the festive period. Secondly, we had to get through Christmas and make it fun for the children at least. Thirdly, my mother in law, who had come over to give us a helping hand, took ill and ended up having to see the hospital doctor. However, the situation for myself was saved when the marvel that is my wife, took herself and the kids to Cornwall as we had planned, for New Year's Day. Thus, I had two days to recuperate. Good thing too as I have to get back to work at some point and the footy kicks off again in a couple of days with training and hopefully a match this Sunday.

Sunday 7th January 2007

Longreach Athletic Reserves versus Avon Plate

Patchway High School
Bristol & District Sunday league Division 4
Referee: No league appointed referee

Team:

Sherry
Bolts Simon Jerry Jumpy
Dr
Ga Yos Korahn Ned
Louis

Subs: James B (for Ga 75 mins)
Daz (unused sub)

Yes, I know what you are thinking, New Year and another shake-up for the Plate line-up. Respect is due to Jerry as he is obviously quite brave to make such bold changes, but he also came over to me and told me that playing right back was not a 'demotion, just that I can play the role'. The Dr going into the holding role was a last minute decision as Reg had failed to turn up. He had gotten 'absolutely pissed and was in no state to play'. No Reg means no Ali because of the lift scenario and the inability to organise an alternative. Not a full squad out today then but thirteen is enough. A quality thirteen to boot. It was a stinker of a day, fine rain, a bit of a wind, sodden pitch and there was no league referee, one of their blokes stepped up to the plate. I was looking out for any negativity which would beat us before we stepped on the pitch but there was none around which I took as a good sign. Now, when I say a 'sodden pitch', I really mean it. There was surface water all over the centre circle and it was only vaguely grassy on the wings. Longreach have a full squad and it is game on for the first time this year.

To say that we start well is an understatement. The first half hour is all Plate. Longreach's best player is in their midfield but the conditions mean that he cannot play his usual game and he falls away. Dr is in the same boat but plays a much more simpler than usual game and is thus more effective. Jumpy and myself actually play the 'pushing on' full back game and squeeze them into their own half. Jerry and Simon are strong at the back. Sherry is certainly looking a good goalkeeper now. Korahn, Louis and Ned are creating havoc up front. Yos is working tirelessly in midfield. We take the lead after a couple of minutes. Ned tackles their defender as he attempts to clear and lifts a beautiful chip over the advancing Longreach 'keeper. By the time five minutes is up, we have created a couple of golden chances and when Louis latches on to a long clearance and copies Ned's chip, we are ecstatic.

We are playing an instinctive game. We find ourselves defending in packs. All of their passes are being intercepted as we simply move in front of them and get our foot in first. Headers are going our way and our attacking trio have more pace than their defence can handle. Plus, it is intensely difficult to turn as a defender when your feet are stuck in the mud. Just about every ball we played or cleared was falling to the young 'uns trio. On fifteen minutes, Louis has another good shot, hits the post with their goalie and defender flailing about in the muddy goalmouth, Korahn is backing up, and standing up, and slots it home. Barely ten minutes later and a Jumpy corner leads to another melee and Ned spins around balettically and finds the ball at his feet and then in the back of the net. As our half hour of dominance comes to a close, we are so dominant that Simon is even getting forward. Another Jumpy cross and Simon leaps like an ageing Salmon (although we can never really know what that looks like as Salmon die after spawning, or are they all old and leaping as they struggle to the spawning grounds?), he is beaten in the air but their chap ever so kindly heads into his own net. 5-0 at this point to the Plate.

It is incredibly enjoyable to play in this match. There are dozens of sliding tackles going in all over the place. The referee is hardly having to do anything though as both teams are trying to play hard-but-fair-but, in atrocious conditions. Having seen the Watford game called off over the festive period, I can tell you that this was worse. In the centre, the ball would hardly run. The best passes of the day were ones you hit as hard as you can and charge after it. When it has moved a full ten feet or so, repeat until hopefully you are whacking it at goal. There was one point where I was just laying on the floor, kicking out all round me as the play went on. I feel sure that this match was reminiscent of some late nineteenth century matches. I did a diving header nice and early, this accustomed me to the wet and cold mud. It certainly was a good idea to get Under Armour 'Cold Gear' for a Christmas present. It did keep me warm and it didn't have that awful feeling of your wet clobber, sloshing around you for ninety minutes.

My one fear at this point in the game, would Longreach try and abandon the match? Unfortunately for them, the rain finally stopped. Just before half time and they get one back from a travesty of defending arts. The ball is played across our goalmouth, Dr leaves it to Jerry who air kicks at the wrong ball, Sherry is stuck in the mud and can only watch as it goes right through to their striker, about two yards out for a tap-in. The last fifteen minutes has been starting to get my calm head dislodged. Plate must have five one on ones and miss them all with wild slices and, 'pitter patter' stuff. I begin to use 'For fucks' sake' more and more. Half time though and 5-1 up. We have managed to play a Sheffield United type game: pressing and harrying, as well as play some okay stuff given the pitch and our finishing has been first class if not consistently clinical. Playing that way comes at a price, especially for an ageing Sunday morning team, that price is feeling absolutely bloomin' knackered. The half time consists of: more communication, keep it positive, hit the ball wide to the only green areas, next goal is vital as this is the sort of day and pitch that anything could happen.

As quite often happens, we decide to do the opposite of what we are told. We keep the ball low, get sloppy, start playing too deep, our shape starts to waver and we cannot get the ball wide or hold onto possession. We are playing into the wind this half, which has conveniently picked up after a lull in the first half (maybe helped us). As the first half was played almost entirely in their half, we are now defending an absolute quagmire. As you can probably tell, 5-1 soon became 5-2 and by sixty five minutes, 5-3. The time seemed to be dragging slowly by. I had not been able to play any sort of pushing on game for a while but now I had to. Our right hand side got back into the groove. Ga was through and smashed a shot against the post, all very exciting. Eventually, we were exerting pressure and the ball fell to me on the edge of the box, I controlled it and took it round their defender. My left leg hurled itself at the ball and it slowly reared up and hit one of their defenders. Thankfully, it fell back to me and I clipped a ball into Louis and he made it 6-3. As we always say, 'In Sunday football, it is always the sixth that is the killer'. No matter what, we had stated our intentions that we were in fact 'up for it' and we did indeed 'want it'. With two minutes remaining, Jerry still had time to smash an attempted clearance into the face of their substitute, the ball falling kindly for them and despatched for a final score of 6-4. Personally, I was over the moon when the final whistle went as I had pelted forward and my calf muscles were beginning to cramp. Daz is now the new Ga as he was a very good linesman / unused substitute. James B came on for the last fifteen minutes or so and provided some much needed fresh legs at the end.

The pub was obviously a great place to be. Most of today's heroes were there. Unfortunately, no landlord and thus no food, we were pretty famished after the exploits of the morning. Plate have 100% record in 2007 and there will be hardly any games played today and so we are likely to march up the table. As well as the usual voting, there also has to be a decision made on the fifth goal scored by the Plate today. Jumpy is claiming it as it was his cross and it was 'going in' before the Longreach player nodded it in. Simon is claiming that he got a touch as he challenged for the header and this was the cause of the goal. However, Simon does not make it to the pub and Jumpy's claims are very tenuous. It was pretty clear that their guy had out jumped Simon and had cleanly headed it into his own net and so in the Plate history it will show an own goal. Even having taken untold throw-ins, my shoulder has held up pretty well and just needs a good soaking in the bath. I have obviously been kicked around the ankles and my left wrist is sore (from falling over probably). Fingers crossed no real niggles.

Man of the Match: Ned – Great goals and first half.
Shirt of Shame: Bolts – Negative when 5-0 up.

You see, this is what I get for caring too much. Do I really want to win too much? I know that some players react badly to being yelled at but by the time we had missed three or four, one-on-one situations, I was getting a bit irate and just needed the team to know that and then move on. I will try and keep it positive. I just get sucked into a vortex when Plate are doing well and then when we revert to type, it bugs me and disappoints me. For me to stop shouting, I would have to lose my desire first. That is why players like Rooney shout and scream at the referees. They probably watch themselves on Match Of The Day and think, 'I will never do that again, it looks so uncool'. However, they carry on because they care and they want to win. Bad enough to win when one is playing crap, but to see perceived injustice, well, it's enough to make the blood boil. I totally condemn abusing refs though. Scream at yourself, scream at your teammates, but not the ref. He/she has enough on their plate without all that nonsense. Scare the referees away and we have no game left. Plus, you will get the odd one who will use his cards and then you are down a player, the referees do not change their minds so there are no winners at all.

A downer when I got home, full of the joys. The wife has been putting off the organising of our weekend away to celebrate our anniversary and I have slowly been bringing up the subject of why. It turns out that she is not happy, that the 'chemistry is not right between us'. She is being 'fatalistic'. We are like the proverbial 'chalk and cheese' and she cannot see us going anywhere. The old chestnut of marijuana was brought up briefly but it was not the time for getting really into it or starting some sort of row. It does help explain my shoulder injury though. Obviously, I knew deep down that something was wrong but didn't communicate it until too late.

Training this week was attended by eighteen players. It made it a little difficult to get into a flow, as there were so many of us. Rather too many than too few that's for certain. Hopefully this means that Jumpy is doing well for money. I have to pay Fry's £330 ASAP and it looks like the kit will finally be ready soon but that has to be paid for.

The sorry tale continues. I had a call just before the Plate Christmas party to say that the printers could rush through the job and have it ready straight away or they could take their time and would be ready on 28th December. I agreed that they shouldn't rush it at this late stage. A window of opportunity to pick up the kit did not arise until the first week of January. The news was not good. The proprietor couldn't understand why we had been told that the kit was ready. I got a bit cheesed off and let my feelings known. I wouldn't leave the shop until he had found out where the disk was and when it was to be finished off. Wednesday tenth January, good enough. Tuesday the ninth of January, I get a call with the boss of the printers asking me what colours we want the logos to be. Now, I thought they were supposed to be ready tomorrow and we have discussed the colours before and oh my goodness can we just get it sorted. Every time I meet up with the team it's, 'Where is the kit?' and have to recite this frustrating tale. I just couldn't be bothered any more so I took it in my stride when I received a call on Friday to say the kit is ready for picking up, tomorrow morning. James B wants his balls paying for and we have the second instalment of the pitch monies to come. The only 'extra' income we will have is when Dan coughs up the £75 he owes and we have a plan to sell off the Argentina/Plate kit to players. There is already great interest but we have to decide on what to do with the most popular numbers (nine, ten etc).

Disaster after the training and pub session were over. The Rome Total War game is causing Yos' computer to crash in the midst of battles. He has a computer genius staying with him this weekend and will hopefully get a solution to this dilemma. I wonder if Yos would splash out the £800 odd that he would need to spend on a new machine that was capable of handling the game. I would if I was in his situation, but with a wife and young kids there is no time to keep up properly with X Boxes and PC games.

Sunday 14th January 2007

Oracle versus Avon Plate

Muller Road Bristol & District Sunday League Division 4

Yet another match bites the dust, should be mud I suppose, as it is the rain that causes another cancellation. The Muller road pitches were played on last weekend and if they were anything like the Patchway pitch ended up last week, then this last week of sheeting rain and constant damp will not be doing the groundsmen any favours.

Last night the wife brought out the big guns as we had another day of rowing and generally not being friendly. The astrological charts were out, as were the tarot cards. As I finished off my joint, I psyched myself up to try and understand and enjoy what was about to happen. As far as I can make out, my chart is showing me to be going through two significant transits. One is to do with Saturn and the other is relating to my Mars / Neptune conjunct, square and trine. Saturn began passing through its transitional house a couple of years ago. At that point I had had a 'nearly affair'. For the next couple of years it will make my subconscious want to escape from the mundanities of life. Unfortunately, at the same time my energy levels (as well as the wife's) will be right down and so the easy option of obliterating myself through weed will be challenged and challenging. Also, the planets shifting round will make me project a motherly, nagging behaviour onto my wife and it will make me rebel against the things that, at the moment, provide our family with security: my job and marriage. I will increasingly have to deal with the fact that I am a server of the greater cause and not a 'star' in my own right; in my marriage I will always put the values of control, stifling and non-ending sacrifice onto my partner. The even greater news is that as my 'mid-life crisis' peters out, the wife's will just be going into the early stages of a four year cycle that will lead to her wanting to bring everything crashing down. The mid-life crisis feelings are as inevitable as, say, being a teenager and the emotions attached to that but once you gain awareness through a medium such as Astrology, one should be able to take more control and stop cycles of destructive behaviours whilst welcoming the more positive ones.

As a sign that my communication skills are improving, I was able to let the wife know when my brain had reached fill-level and was taking in no more. You must understand that I am reading Stephen Hawking's 'A Brief History of Time' and thus there is a conflict in my head of Astronomy versus Astrology. Although I do believe in what the missus describes and see so much of it in me that it cannot be ignored. Then it was onto the tarot. I made sure that I caught up on the Derby result that I had missed earlier due to a visit to the SS Great Britain (Derby win again 1-0 versus Sheffield Wednesday to now be level at the top of the Championship with Birmingham City) before asking the cards to look at the future of my marriage. I swear every card was on the theme of being faced with the choices of a life which accepts change and evolution. Examples of the cards that appeared in the spread were:
Five of Wands – 'A time of struggle where the individual must battle with the dragon of material reality...mundane matters may begin to go wrong and more attention must be paid to the demands and limits of concrete reality.'
Ten of Wands – 'the individual is overburdened and oppressed by having taken on more than he or she can deal with. The imagination has been stifled by too many worldly concerns... certain things may need to be relinquished so that the creative process can be refreshed and a new cycle may begin.'

Four of Pentacles – 'An attitude of holding too tightly to things which are bound up with one's sense of self-value. The fear of loss may mean no loss, but it also means no gain.'
Thankfully: Two of pentacles – 'Heralds a time when money and energy are likely to be available for new projects that might lead to a rewarding future; but the individual must be willing to put his resources to work, taking risks and using capital, rather than hoarding and saving at a time when new opportunities arise.'
Tellingly, the 'significator' was: The Hanged Man – ' augers the need for a voluntary sacrifice for the purpose of acquiring something of greater value…in the hopes of a new and better life.'

The question I asked the cards was to do with the future of my marriage. Looking through the whole book of card-meanings, there are plenty which more than hint that the relationship you are in is doomed. Stop deluding yourself and get the hell out there is suggested by several of the cards. Thankfully, I didn't pick any of those out which gives a bit of hope. With the other half talking about the need for change in our relationship and dealings with each other, it is telling that so many of the cards in my spread suggest the need for change and 'letting go' of what I have relied on for so long.

Along with the Astrology, everything is pointing to several mischiefs: A mid life crisis, which will then be followed by the wife's. That if I am lax with work because of my need to escape its servile nature and it being seen as a chain round my neck, I will lose everything. It seems that my insistence on holding onto my marijuana-smoking ways and being so into footy/sport in general (when it affects family life) is to be challenged. It is difficult to even imagine myself without weed, lots of footy and sport involvement and the desire to have time on my own. It means spending more time out of my imagination and in the 'real world'. When the missus brought up my football cravings, such as preparing for the Derby results on a Saturday, when this is supposed to be our only full day together as a family, it surprised me as billions of people worldwide face similar dilemmas every week, it is part of manhood the world over. It comes down to how much she can accept.

To my mind, I will play football and cricket until my body packs up. Hopefully at least one of the kids will be into football and then I can live that life with them whilst developing our father-child relationship and getting out and about. I am still going to pack in the club secretary role at the Plate and I am just a player with the cricket team. I will try and cut down on watching Saturdays' 'Gillette Soccer Special' and accept that Saturdays are for family and not primarily for Derby County supporting although I will keep it up as much as possible of course.

I have had thoughts about kicking up a stink at work because of their pay-reduction threat. However, I had already quashed those thoughts in a self-preservation stylie and to keep up a good income for the family. I have not had any thoughts of trying to escape the marriage through an affair that is what may well have happened in the past. One thing I must try and do, for my own sanity's sake as well as for the good of the relationship, is to stop thinking that every time my wife asks me a question, she is not trying to 'trick me', or 'catch me out' or 'give me chores to do if I am not 100% busy'. Whilst I put this mother-son type relationship on us, it will never work. Any inheritance I am due from my Grandpa's 'estate' will probably account for the influx of money. Whenever I have had money in the past, I have used it to play the stock market or use as deposits for houses so I am quite good at using money rather than just saving it at which I am rubbish. Can't wait for a boost to my energy levels too.

No training for me this week because the missus had an Astrological supervision. We couldn't get a babysitter because we needed her mother to look after the children so that we could go out for our fourth wedding anniversary 'celebration'. Although it started quite poorly, not much chat and what there was had a little tension in there. I'm sure it is quite usual for couples to get around to the core of an issue in as roundabout a way as possible. Taking their time, and making the road to understanding as rocky as possible. So we did that for a while and then it seemed to crystallize. We seem to be at a point where we are on two parallel paths. This is necessary because we are both trying to find our way and our path forward. However we 'evolve' as people at this time will determine what we want / need for a long time to come. I am very up and down in my feelings about all this. As part of my wife's needs is to deal with the 'almost' affair I had when Louis was four months old. This has led to a hardening of her heart and less desire to make herself vulnerable again. Already, I am having arguments in my head about the validity of her feelings here. In myself I know that I am, 'cured' of that sort of behaviour or desire. We both agreed at the time that I was destined to do it, partly due to the fact that part of my make up is decided by my father. Thankfully, it never became any sort of full-blown affair, and it was two and a half years ago. On the other hand, I, of course, accept that there were texts involved and that if not physically, then mentally it was a betrayal. Also, I have the great need for physical love. Holding hands, cuddles and sex. I know myself, and I can see me getting quite sulky and resentful. It is something I must fight.

There is big news this week which is concerning millions of us worldwide. Is it: the fallout from the BBC's 'Climate Week'? No, this is only concerned with global catastrophe and the massive chunks of Antarctica that keep falling into the sea as the ice melts. Is it: The way in which Tony Blair's morally and philosophically bankrupt reign is unravelling in the lead up to his 'long goodbye.'? No, this is not new news, surely most people knew that as he lost his dictatorial-type power, his legacy would be a few good uses of the press with nothing to back up this 'don't upset the middle class especially but upset none if possible (i.e. do nothing except pander to the tabloid editors and not try and build something tangible or challenging.)'. Is it: The continuing mismanagement of the 'War on Terrorism'? No, we will have the occasional laugh when it comes to US election times and then let them get on with it. No, of course it is the downfall of the dim-witted, ignorant, abhorrent creation of the Chavs known as Jade Goody.

As befits this crazy modern-world we live in, Jade has been built up into a 'mega-celebrity' because she is worshipped by all the other 'ladies' who see any form of celebrity as 'success'. No matter how stupid you are made out to look, no matter how crass you are portrayed, no matter how many people you have hurt or let down, as long as you are getting your picture in the paper everything is cool. She is a role model to all those who don't want to earn their success, they want to able to open a supermarket or appear in yet another 'I'm A Celebrity And Want To Stay One' reality show. Everyone knows that Jade is a complete fuck-up as a human being. Her social skills appear minimal, she can hold no conversation whatsoever, she is a liar (selling fitness videos when you've had liposuction), she is incredibly ugly because of her permanent scowl and false breasts that are somehow balanced on her chest, she has few morals and chases the paparazzi so that it's them complaining of harassment. However, this time she has done something really awful. Appearing on Big Brother once again is bad enough, but now, she is the ringleader of a racist bullying group who have picked on the Bollywood superstar: Shilpa Shetty. Effigies are being burnt in India; the program backers (The Carphone Warehouse) are pulling the plug on their sponsorship of the show. There are campaigns in the papers to evict Ms Goody because she is depicting the British as a vile and racist mob. Even the Sun newspaper are harping on about how dreadful it is of her to say things like calling her 'Shilpa Poppadom' and should 'go back to where she came from' or 'spend a day in the slums' and so on. The Sun, I mean come on, there is hypocrisy and there is blatant hypocrisy and the Sun's is bloomin' blatant.

As you may have gathered, I have no sympathy for Jade Goody and I hope that this is the end for her and her shameful ways;

hopefully it will be the end of the celebrity-dominated society that we live in. Hopefully it will signal a return to earning stardom with talent or hard graft rather than getting your tits out, shagging around and getting your picture taken. I hope it will signal a return to the youth wanting to get an education rather than ending up such a miserable oaf as Jade. Maybe 'Hello' and their ilk will donate some of their future profits to anti-racist campaigns. Maybe the Sun will watch its own racism in future as it will become obvious in future and they may be attacked too. Unfortunately the Sun rag is overpriced by about thirty pence per day so I wont be keeping a close eye on them but hopefully some people will.

One thing that I think will come out of this is the end of Big Brother and other reality shows as the entity it has become. A social experiment in an enclosed environment is interesting, educational and would reveal something of the human condition. However, this system of picking the most disparate group who are selected for their inability to mix and tendency to rage has become a sad joke. The Jade stuff has all blown up because the producers knew what they were doing in setting this group up for the show. The editing then made the argument and the racism seem to flow like a fine wine at a bankruptcy convention. It is strange, that whilst the rest of the world protests and gnashes its teeth, in the house they are quite unaware of any great trouble and the day after this all blew up, the editing was concentrated on the contestants saying that nothing was said in a racist way. So, what seems to be happening is that people are now criticising the makers of the show and that can only be a good thing.

One thing is for certain; the reaction is totally out of context to the situation. PC persons want us to believe that racism is a 'disease' that can be 'cured' through knowledge and cultural mixing pots. In my view, the simple fact is that human nature has been developed as we have evolved down from the trees. One of our traits is to worry when we see persons that are different from ourselves as they will be a threat to resources such as food, shelter and territory. This is deep rooted in us and we can reduce it through education and exposure, but it will never go away. In the Victorian era they tried it with emotions, the stiff upper lip and domination of children, but that failed. The 1930's USA they tried it with the base urges to booze, they failed miserably too. In modern times, society is trying it with drugs and the human trait to obtain as much pleasure out of a resource as possible, and they are failing in that too. Of course, through history, Christianity has taken on most of our evolved, base drives and failed utterly (especially when it comes to their own priests and other holy men).

Sunday 21st January 2007

Cutters Friday Reserves versus Avon Plate

Cutters Club, Stockwood Lane
Bristol & District Sunday League Division 4

The furore over Celebrity Big brother should be over now. Hopefully with a return to the climate matters. The storm known as Kyrill, which struck our shores over the last week and killed ten, has also led to yet another postponed match due to a waterlogged pitch. There was an inspection at teatime Saturday. There was standing water on the pitch and the groundsman couldn't use his line-marking machine. The disappointment was mixed with a certain amount of relief. As there will be bugger all games going on this weekend, Cutters would surely have been playing a good many of their most highly rated players. Also, it transpires that Korahn would have been away as he is in America doing some skating. As we have already played them once this season, there is little chance of a double-header fixture coming up later in the season, when the league will have to catch up on all these missed fixtures. Annoyingly, the cup matches will now keep coming up until they are resolved, and there are teams in our division that will be involved and this will lead to more league cancellations.

Thank goodness for Yos. He rang to invite me out to watch Arsenal versus Manchester United at the Plough. I was feeling really low, thinking over all the information with regards my marriage. For some reason, I felt very lonely and it was nice to be remembered and wanted. When I telephoned the wife to tell her I would be out, I realised that I was on the edge of tears. A few beers, footy, joints, computer game (now playing my 'Medieval Total War' because of the trouble Yos' computer was having with the other version) all steadied my mind but I still had a quite sleepless night.

The Bangles once squeaked out a tune called, 'Just Another Manic Monday'. I had one of those this week that goes to show, once again, that I must give up the Club Secretary role at the end of this season.

After all that I had several Plate jobs to do: arrange the team members who will represent the Plate at this Wednesday's league meeting at the Memorial Ground. I usually go, but the wife works Wednesday evenings so I am with the children. Next, organise the selling off of the Argentina kit to raise much needed funds for the Plate (£20 gets you the shirt of your choice, after that the price will go down until they are all gone. The chance to own a piece of Plate history is too good a chance to miss and I will certainly be having the number two shirt). I then had to contact Frys Club to talk to their guy about the still unpaid pitch bill and book us a pitch for a match this coming Sunday. They actually played matches at Frys on Saturday but none on Sunday as the pitches needed to recover .So there is hope for a game for us this weekend. I needed to double-check the February weekend that I have 'closed' with the league. If it is on the date I think it is then I can do my wife a big favour. It was necessary to ensure that a registration form was in my bag so that we can sign up a new boy: Patrick. It is great timing for him to come on board. He does look a class centre back and Si has played his last game for the Plate this season as he has moved to St Ives in Cornwallshire. Emails had to be sent to remind Sherry to bring Plate funds with him on Thursday. Finally an email was sent to update the team on the weekend's games and details of the opposition where we should be playing next Sunday.

A mad dash to training after Louis' third birthday 'party'. It is warming to see him with a day that is special to him. The twins always share a birthday and Christmas is for all. My mum has also come down for her yearly visit. It is all a bit much for me at the moment. My thoughts are tired from thinking about my marriage and work and Plate stuff, I don't seem to have any mental energy left for my mum. However, training was one of those times when everything goes well for one. Yos and I were driving each other on in midfield until we had completely dominated. There were twenty players there. The opposition had the two young 'uns who had made it but they also had three non-Platers in their team. There was a no-show from Jerry who has to do his tax returns for the 31st January deadline. With the experience and wiliness of our old heads, our team actually played with some shape as well as a bundle of energy and we earned the right to start playing some wonderful one and two touch football. Soon, the non-Platers began to get some stick as they weren't busting a gut, or communicating well or tracking back etc. in the days when the Plate were struggling for numbers, these players were a God-send, now however, they may begin to hold us back. Twenty players was just about the maximum that our training pitch can handle. What a turnaround to be in the position of needing to ask non-Platers to stop coming on a Thursday. I breezed back in to our house later on thinking this had been one of my greatest ever football showings, as far as a training session can be counted (which is not very much), but the feeling one gets from receiving the ball and knowing where you are going to put it before you take any touch, and then seeing it go exactly where you wanted at the right pace, lovely. What a pity that Jer wasn't there. Yos and myself would have been cast-iron certainties for centre midfield on Sunday.

In the pub afterwards, the new kit was premiered and went down extremely well. It is a rather lovely affair and well worth the strife and the cost in getting it. Plans are being formulated for a press release and we have a photographer coming on Sunday to take some glorious action shots. Sherry was able to give me some Plate cash so that I can now cover the first pitch bill of £330. We have another of those to come plus we have to pay a few more quid in league fees and have an AGM and trophies to pay for. The sale of the Argentina kit is definitely going ahead and it looks like we have a few takers already although for maybe a little less than the hoped for £20 each.

As a Derby County fan in 'exile', with a young family, and rarely in a comfortable financial position, it means that I had not been to their new home at Pride Park. I have lost count of the amount of time I have to tell the story of why I haven't been to the new ground when I am so obviously a fan. Now, however, I have cracked my Pride Park cherry. When the Rams drew Bristol Rovers in the FA Cup the opportunity arose. Within the Plate there are Rovers fans of course and there is also myself and Ga who are Rams fans. Ga was already going up to Derby to get some furniture for his new abode so I could get a lift with him and a mate. In the Rovers car was Dave and DJ James and, as they want to play for the Plate tomorrow, they are coming back after the match and I can get a lift with them. Also, the tickets are a reduced-price £16 which is manageable with no travel expenses on top.

Thankfully, we arrived at the ground early and so had time to have a stroll right round the stadium. It couldn't help but make a Derby fan proud to have such a glorious home. One with decent toilets to boot. After some lubrication at the bar, we watched the players warming up. It is so exciting to watch these 'gods' in the flesh. Respect is due to both sets of fans; the Rovers end was packed with 6,000 of their screaming horde and the crowd topped 25,000. I obviously watched a different match to the one witnessed by the media. The play of Derby has moved on light years from the fare served up a few years ago when I last was able to see them on a regular basis. Play being switched from side to side, back heels and flicks, passes on the ground and to feet. Even though Billy Davies had made some changes to the last matches line-up, the squad looks very strong. We had Michael Johnson back in central defence for the suspended Leacock. Seth Johnson and Bob Malcolm replaced Jones and Pearson in centre midfield. New-boy, Gary Teale was cup-tied and Lupoli came in to start. Richard Jackson was in for Edworthy.

In my view, Derby had the obvious talent and passing moves. Rovers were excellent at getting good crosses into our box and they won most of the second ball. It is true that they created the scariest moments. We were sat behind the goal being defended by Derby in the first half, thus, we saw Bywater make some world-class saves, especially from a short-range header. A near back-pass / own goal didn't help matters. However, I didn't sense any tension in the air really and there seemed only the possibility that they might make us have to beat them in a replay (which I could have attended even easier). Once they had a man sent off with about twenty minutes to go, they were doomed. The excellent Seth set up Peschisolido for a cracking finish with about ten minutes to go. Derby continued to look solid enough and held out for the win.

I do hope that Seth Johnson earns a new contract. He was tremendous for us in his first stint with us before being sold to Leeds for enough to pay for our Academy and training complex. He came back to us when he was eventually released and didn't seem to quibble about the wages we could offer him. At the time he arrived, Derby had been in the doldrums for a while as it became increasingly obvious that the club was being run in an ad-hoc fashion, Burley had gone and promotion seemed to slipping out of our dreams once more. So to get a big-name player was refreshing. His contract is up in the summer but he has said he wants to stay and try and win his place in the squad. On today's showing, he must be impressing Billy.

Coming back, my Rovers pals were chatty for about half an hour, thanks largely to booze. Any chat soon gave way to the silence induced by the end of the Wembley dream for them. Occasionally there would be a burst of singing from the back and I didn't stop smiling for the three-hour journey home.

Sunday 28th January 2007

Avon Plate versus R & P Wonderboys

Frys Club Bristol & District Sunday League Division 4
Referee: G Miles (league appointed)

Team:

Sherry
Bolts Patrick Si Jumpy
Dr
DJ James Yos Korahn Ned
Louis

Subs: Jer (for DJ James 70 mins)
Daz (for Jumpy 70 mins)
Dave (for Yos 80 mins)
Reg (Linesman)
Ali (unused sub)

After a full week of dry weather it is game on. The first subject to discuss is their team name. It may well say 'Old Boys' in their title now, originally however, they seem to have been called the R & P 'Wonderboys'. This is, you will agree, a dreadful name. They also play in an all yellow kit. We, on the other hand, have a wonderful name and we have the first match in our new kit. It is sheer quality. It feels silky to the touch and hangs wonderfully, even on our torsos. Half the trick with Premiership stars must be their kit. It feels like having quality equipment will improve us.

Today, I am also wearing a pair of prototype Adidas Predators. I have hardly worn them because I love my Puma Kings, but also because they are blue, but what the hell. With an Under Armour, 'Cold Gear' t-shirt, and a headband by the same manufacturer, I feel the business and up for the battle ahead. Their points total is worse than ours and so by all accounts they appear doomed. To give R & P some hope, Avon Plate have not won at home this season at all. This outfit have a bit of a 'tough-guy' reputation which are the sort of teams that can catch us out, we have a proper referee today so that should stop any of that nonsense. The referee inadvertently helped me out today. He came into the changing room and said that he would only tolerate bad language if you were swearing at yourself. At any other time, and you were off. My worst habit is the negative swearing that I get into once wound up or frustrated. I was able to prepare myself in a cooler and more calculated fashion. As you will notice once again, there is a change to our line-up. The DJ is in for Ga. Perhaps more significantly is Jer for debutante Patrick. He is, of course, our new-boy who has been to training several times and obviously knows the game, is big and tall, tackles well, is quick, communicates, good in the air and with the ball at his feet. It is such great timing with this being Si's last match before moving to Cornwall. It gives Jer the chance to watch from the sidelines for a bit and see a game from that perspective.

We kick off with a slight wind behind us and annoyingly long grass tugging at our studs (or blades as in my case today). Within two minutes there is a worry. DJ James has a long shot which is arrowing into the top corner; their 'keeper somehow dives full length across his goal and catches the ball. A top 'keeper can make all the difference and looking at their record, they have not lost any games by a large margin. In the Plate's first ever game, we fielded a semi-pro 'keeper and won 1-0. We proceeded to lose most of the rest of our early games by massive scores with only the goalkeeper having changed. It soon becomes clear that we have a very healthy advantage in terms of the young 'uns speed versus their ageing and not particularly svelte defence. With Yos working hard, Ned creating problems, and DJ James having one of his best games we are pulling them about at will. Meanwhile, at the back we are totally spoilt with two centre-backs who obviously know what they are doing and chatting away to Jumpy and myself. This tends to make us play a little more defensive but we were solid and the front boys were causing enough merry hell on their own. The Dr, Jumpy and myself were buzzing around our centre halves and with our distribution and experience we had a great balance and options.

So it was that after just six minutes, a corner into their box led to a scramble and an overhead kick from Patrick and he is off the mark. A spectacular debut so far. Certainly not the first time a Plater has scored on their debut but I am not sure how many of them were centre backs. Louis is having an absolute blinder of a game except for just one point, the ball will not go in the back of their net from his shots. He is through on goal several times and their excellent 'keeper saves them all. We have to wait until the twenty fifth minute for Korahn to pick up the ball and smash it straight over the 'keeper and in. 2-0 to the Plate and we are rampant. Eventually, I almost start swearing because it almost looks as if our blokes are having a mess about in front of goals with too many passes and wayward shooting. Ten minutes before the interval and for the first time in the match, the R & P forwards are able to produce some slick passing and one of their chaps runs off his marker and slots a goal back to 2-1. There are a nervy few minutes before the half time whistle blows.

R & P are not a bad team. Their delivery of corners has been excellent. If they get room they can play but we are not giving them any room. The Dr is switched into a two-man front pairing as we are holding them so easily and need some clinical finishing. I decide that the second half will see a more forward playing, pushing on right back. After all, as I see it, we play a pushing on full back game to take risks but to push back other teams and stop us defending too deep. Amidst all the backslapping and motivational talk, I am glad that noone can mind read. Secretly I am dreading a half of grim hard work, one of the exceedingly few times this thought has come up. I cannot help feeling that we are going to continue to squander chances and they will score a couple of scrappy ones and win.

The pattern of the second half is very similar to the first. Their dead ball delivery remains exemplary but Cris is excelling in our goal. His punches and flaps are doing enough to put the R & P forwards off their stride. We clear at least two more corner-created efforts off the line with Jumpy and I on the posts. They have a small share of possession but do not threaten from open play, especially with Si and Patrick winning all the headers. The only ray of hope they receive comes from one of our back-passes that Cris manages to air-kick and their guy is through, but he screws his shot across goal and I am there to clear up the mess. Meanwhile, the mayhem at the other end has gathered pace with the introduction of the Dr up there. Although things never get too tense for us, I am thrilled when our third goes in. It is Patrick again. Again from a corner that led to a scramble. This time it is a 'chicken-leg' from about a yard out.

To finish R & P off, Jer makes a double substitution, bringing himself on for DJ James and Daz on for Jumpy. The last twenty minutes is now all us. They use subs as well but we have brought on damn fine players where they are changing just for fresh legs to replace knackered ones. Daz makes a few telling contributions: With about quarter of an hour to go, he threads a lovely ball to the Dr who passes it under the 'keeper and in for our fourth goal. Daz then decides to show his goalkeeping skills. Cris has parried an attempt which arose from another of the R & P corners, the ball is dribbling towards the post and Daz throws himself down and makes sure the ball goes outside of the post by palming it for another corner. Indignation and disbelief from both sets of players as the referee waves away the appeals for a penalty. At this point, the need for a proper referee comes to the fore. Their sideline-manager gets very hot under the collar about the non-penalty and the general hammering they are taking. Eventually, the guy has to be sent from the pitch. Of course, if the ref had done his job properly in the first place, the situation shouldn't have arisen. Once the problem has occurred though, you need the referee to quell it. Jer further distracts the referee from reconsidering his decision by substituting Yos for Dave and to rub salt into the wound, Plate decide to put together one last move. Dr crosses for Ned to nod back the ball from the far post and Korahn's left foot does the rest. 5-1 to the Plate and the score line flatters R & P.

Pheasant casserole down the pub after the match. Only trouble is, it takes so long to prepare and cook, that most of the team have had to shoot off before it arrives. We have a quiet word that we are hungry at one o'clock let alone at four o'clock. Something simpler and quicker would be our ideal. However, the landlord has this tradition of running a soup kitchen for locals and at the same time practising his culinary skills, which are immense I'm sure. A good sign is Patrick coming down the boozer. There is a tinge of sadness as Si has played his last game for us for this and possibly for any season. He is coming for a drink on Thursday after training so any tears can wait until then. The voting went as you might expect:
Shirt of shame: Daz – forgetting he was not the goalkeeper
Man of the match: - Patrick for his all round excellent debut.
Our first win at home. Our 100% record for 2007 is still intact. We have finally managed to win as many games as we have lost this season. In fact, as we have reached the half waypoint in our fixtures it is worth having a look at the table:

Team	Played	Won	Drawn	Lost	For	Against	Goal difference	Points
Brislington 1987	10	8	2	0	52	12	+40	26
Warwick	9	8	0	1	42	12	+30	24
Portcullis	8	5	2	1	24	15	+9	17
Northville	11	5	1	5	28	31	-3	16
Avon Plate	**11**	**5**	**1**	**5**	**35**	**39**	**-4**	**16**
Cutters Friday	11	4	1	6	19	28	-9	13
Oracle	10	4	0	6	22	17	+5	12
South Bristol	6	3	1	2	18	20	-2	10
R & P	11	3	1	7	18	27	-9	10
Longreach	8	3	0	5	20	33	-13	9
Farmhouse	9	2	0	7	15	23	-8	7
Queenshead	10	2	0	8	14	50	-36	6

Training was nothing short of hard work. Players like myself have had their fitness levels diminished by the 'monsoon season' break. I started badly, as did my team-for-the-night and then proceeded to get steadily worse. I also managed to take a clearance smack in the face. Shouts would come for me to cover the centre whilst I am struggling to breathe through my bleeding nose. Eventually I had to swallow a rather large lump of clotted blood, which still makes me shudder now. There is blood everywhere and players are asking me if I know that I have a nosebleed. 'Really?'

It was sad to say goodbye to Simon. Great player, great mate, funny guy, always there at Plate socials and holidays. On the pitch he was a great communicator who did not get flustered easily. Not blessed with searing pace, he was a great reader of the game. Superb in the air but with the desire for us as a team to try and play with the ball on the deck and not to panic. His dry humour quite often cut me back down to size when I was getting out of hand. He possessed most of the attributes that I couldn't show at training tonight.

Incredibly, out of our initial squad, we have had seven drop out: Craig (who inexplicably dropped off the radar), Lewis (friend of Craig so dropped out at the same time), Ross (the other chum of Craig in our team), Joff (head quite woozy and too busy living a life that includes late Saturday nights), Drew (constantly injured and thus retired), Dan (fell out of love with the game after our first match fiasco), and now Si. In their place have come: Ned (young 'un with good football-brain), Tyler (not yet a regular but is certainly good enough), Tony (was coming along regularly until his work has taken him away but no reason he shouldn't come back), and now Patrick (who for this coming Sunday was supposed to be working but wangled it so that he could play). Hopefully, we are at a settled stage with regards the squad, just as professional teams are dealing with the closing of the transfer window.

Sunday 4th February 2007

Avon Plate versus Queens Head Rangers

Frys Club, Keynesham Bristol & District league Division 4
Referee: No league appointed referee

Team:

Sherry

Bolts Patrick Reg Jumpy

Dr

Ali Yos Ga Ned

Louis

Subs: DJ James B (referee 1st half on for Louis half time)

Although the pitch is still white with frost, the recent cold snap is, of course, replaced by a bright, dry and windless Sunday morning. The only fly in the ointment being that neither Lee nor Korahn are coming today and they were going to referee the match as they are carrying knocks. With Dave, Jerry, Daz, Tony and Tyler not being available either, I am having to use too much brain-power on the referee / linesman / ringing round players and not on concentrating on getting myself focussed for the match ahead. Things are eased when the Queens Head boys turn up. They only have ten men and they seem as good a bunch as I remember from our last encounter. Queens Head lost 2-10 last week to Northville but they only had eight men that time. Last time we played them we had no ref and no trouble, so there is acceptance from both sides that we will do our best and see what happens.

With Jerry being off sick, Yos has the dubious pleasure of picking the team and tactics. Luckily for him we have the fewest numbers for a while and so he will not have to leave anyone out. He does have the referee problem though. With Ali being rather hesitant, Yos makes the decision for DJ James to ref the first half with Ali taking his usual position on the right. I am slightly surprised that Ga goes in centre midfield with me staying at right back but I'm certainly not going to give him any grief when he has organising to do early on a Sunday morning. Thankfully, Patrick did manage to wangle his shifts so that he can be here today. It is uncertain who our first choice centre back partnership will eventually be, but it is Reg's turn to have a go today. Keeping the Dr as a holding midfielder as well as a back four, against ten men mind you, seems a little conservative for Yos but we seem up for it and the strength of the squad means that although there are lots of changes and absences once more, we can cope and look strong still.

Within two minutes we have a chance. Yos receives the ball, in space, in their box. He has time to steady himself and unleashes a fierce shot, wide. Our usual top scorer is still on one for the season. Keep plugging away, the goals will surely come mate. Still inside the first five minutes and Louis has good possession on the edge of their penalty area. A shot along the floor and the groans are beginning to well. We saw him do so many of these type shots last week. Hang on though, this week the ball slips under their 'keeper and it is in. 1-0 to the Avon Plate.

Often, the danger of playing ten men is that the ten tend to step up a gear. There is a bonding created through shared adversity. The pressure is off as they now have a ready-made excuse for defeat but a heroic tale to tell if they win or draw. Meanwhile, the team of eleven decide that they can win at a canter due to their numerical advantage. The opposition that have turned up are discounted and complacency sets in. If this is the best ten that the opposition have and they have the temporary boost to team spirit, then you are in trouble. There is also the strange quirk in football that if you start off sloppily and with a slow tempo, it is very difficult to then inject the urgency that you require.

On this particular day, the eleven men are closing down as hard as they can. It is the eleven men who are playing as a team and it is the eleven men who are showing they are more up for it. Unfortunately, for the next twenty minutes we create an awful lot of half chances as well as damn good chances, and spurn the lot. Things are not too worrying as we have them completely snuffed out as an attacking force. Their lone striker is beautifully marshalled by Reg and Patrick. Jumpy and myself are used to the pushing on game now and there is tons of space and loads of ball where we are. Apart from the first twenty minutes, there is really no challenge to our flanks as they retreat deeper into their own half. Although they have ten men, it seems to be seven or eight as our passing game is tearing them apart. We have three good players in the centre plus Patrick can get in there for headers so that area of the park is also ours. With Louis' pace and trickery, we dominate the whole pitch. Rare though it is, when Sherry is called upon, he is immaculate.

Frustration turns to relief and to joy for the final twenty minutes of the first half. A ball in from Ned on the left is headed partially clear by the Queens' defence, it falls to the edge of the box and on the half-volley it is Yos who scores, again, under their 'keeper. His is definitely a face etched in relief. As often happens, one leads to two. Another cross from Ned goes near post where it loops up and over the goalie to the unmarked Yos at the far post to nod in. 3-0 to Plate.

On our left we have Jumpy and Ned who are having a great time. On my flank, I was finding it difficult to work with Ali who has played very few games, but we still managed several nice interchanges and produced lots of ball into the final third. It encourages me to move forward even more and I get a lot of possession but my crosses are either not of the highest quality or the ones I plonk straight onto Platers' heads are off target. Back to the left and we have a glorious few minutes of witnessing Jumpy on the rampage. Our fourth and fifth goals follow one after the other. Both from the right boot of our left back. They look identical to me but he is able to tell me of many discerning features for both. One was farther out, one curled more whereas the other was simply smashed into the roof of the net. 5-0. With the last kicks of the half, Louis decides to go on a mazy dribble and, with the option of squaring to our increasingly striker-like right full back, he instead slips the ball in at the near post with a cheeky little chip over their goalkeeper. Half time and it's 6-0 to Avon Plate.

The change of referee at the interval and we all promise more of the same with even more passing please. Inevitably, we start the second half in a sloppy and casual fashion. Unfortunately for Queens Head, this is a lull which only means that they are slightly under the cosh rather than overwhelmed. After experiencing several breakdowns in possession on the edge of their box, the frustration starts to creep in again. At half time, my thoughts were concerned with the fact that Avon Plate have never scored ten goals in a single game and we had reached over half way. Queens Head were bound to tire in the second half and so it was definitely on. Our start to the half had made my tendency to shout negatively appear. It is by no means all moans and groans. I try and communicate all the time and when others stop, or the shape is going, I feel it is up to the senior players such as myself to get things back on track. Sometimes, some negative attacks come out but on a footy pitch, nothing is a personal attack, just a thought said in the heat of a battle situation. I also have to deal with the impatience caused by Father Time's relentless pursuit for the ending of my 'football career'. If I was thirty-five, I would look at the likes of Korahn and the other young 'uns and think that they would be getting stronger and more experienced over the next couple of years. Ally this to their undoubted talent and I would be looking forward to five years of promotions and cup glories. As it is, I only have a couple of seasons left in me I reckon. Thus, I am in an extreme hurry to win some sort of medals as a player.

After ensuring that my area of defence was totally won, I began creeping further forward. The Dr was getting a bit twitchy about not having scored and began pushing on. Ga was used to his position and began creating through the centre with Yos still dominant. Ali had moved up top and looked more comfortable. DJ James was in his usual position and gave us good width on the right.

As the half settled down, we hit a rhythm of playing and scoring. Ned got the goals flowing again after a long pass from Yos set him through. It looked like he had taken too long but, in his usual fashion, calmly slotted into the corner. Yos became a hat-trick hero with our eighth goal. Yos certainly owes Ned a beer or two. DJ James crossed too far but Ned chased the lost cause and managed pull the ball back for Yos to control and pass it in. Ned was also partly responsible for the goal which gave Ga his first of the season.

All the while, I was charging from back to front almost constantly. Whenever we lost possession (not often) and I would turn to head back, I would look up and Plate had the ball back. For some reason, I was ignored a good many times and I was thinking about the big ten goals challenge and that we had to do it. So I decided to play as a forward. Thinking back now, I had a few chances to shoot but didn't. My first real chance came from a ball into the box that, when my head connected, led me to start a shout of 'yes, get in aaarrgghh'. My head had been thrown at the ball, it was on target yet somehow their goalkeeper appeared from nowhere and pushed it round the post. Finally, and it felt inevitably, Plate scored the important tenth goal. A corner was coming over, a Queens Head defender tried to get his baldhead in the way, taking the gamble on him missing it, our no.2 got on the edge of the six-yard area and met it with his head. Forehead onto shoulder (ball kept on the same trajectory though) and in. 'At last' I screamed as I wheeled away.

Avon Plate have possibly played thirty or so games in our history where we have not been able to field eleven players. As well as the possible benefits there is a flip side to this: It is incredibly disheartening. You feel a bit embarrassed before the kick off and can start the game on a damage limitation exercise. As Plate found, as we were already a close bunch of friends, the adversity can produce a long-lasting spirit. It can also break teams. Respect is due to Queens Head that they did not get shirty. They were obviously disappointed and did not put up a great fight but they kept on battling right up to the 89th minute. At this point they had nothing left and Ali was able to nip in and snatch the ball of their defence and slashed it in to score his debut goal and make the final score 11-0 to Avon Plate.

The Greenbank is the place to celebrate. 100% record in 2007 still, now two wins on the spin at home, we are now in positive goal difference for the first time this season, we have won more games than we have lost, we kept a clean sheet, a record victory and the first with us hitting double figures. Another celebration follows as the manager has made lovely sandwiches, which are ready when we are. The glory is relived. We struggle to think of Shirt of Shame moments. It is very heart-warming to see the young 'uns so excited by the Golden Boot standings. I keep records of the season's stats and it is close in the scoring charts. It is an endictment of the way the professional top teams have treated the domestic cups over the past few years. The young 'uns want to discount all the cup goals as they are not as meaningful. These boys watch Match of the Day and try to emulate the stars in many ways. Taking only league goals into consideration the scorers chart stands thusly:
Dr – 9
Louis – 8

Korahn – 7
Ned – 6
Yos – 4
Bolts – 3
Jumpy / Patrick – 2
Lee / DJ James / Ali / Ga – 1
Three goals for me then, but my mantra is: 'Must shoot more'.

The fourth of the Argentina shirts is sold for £20 (to Ga) and Sherry announces that he already has £210 in the coffers. Jumpy may even have £50 or so from the excess training funds at the end of the season. Looks like the Plate are going to do all right on and off the pitch.
Shirt of Shame: Reg – shouting 'No' and changing his mind as a goal went in.
Man of the Match: Jumpy – two corking goals

As for my ageing self, it is lovely to not think about turning my knee over until after matches when I suddenly remember the pain and stress of the last seven seasons since the ligament snapped and then healed properly so slowly. (Playing practically every game for ninety minutes more often than not and with not much alternative rehab going on didn't help the healing process it must be admitted). I ache in many places, hamstrings and shoulders mostly, but then I ran much more than usual today. Sure, if I sit still for half an hour, my back aches and okay, if I kneel onto my left knee the pain is excruciating sharp and my shoulder blades give me gip at the least opportunity but instead of feeling my age, as I have since the enforced weather and Christmas break, now the feelings are of feeling fitter again and, although the period of recovery after a game is getting greater, there are no injury worries (touch wood touch wood again) and that I have several (three?) more seasons in me. If this turns out to be the case it would mean putting on hold the moving to Cornwall plans for a little longer. They have been appearing quite seductive to me in recent times.

I wasn't finished with sport for the day. After nipping off to score another type of result, it was to Sherry's for a bit of the Wales v Ireland rugby before finally going to The Plough Public House for a Cowboys cricket meeting. There is a very exciting tournament being planned by the Easton Cowboys organisation. There is to be an alternative football world cup, an alternative 20:20 cricket world cup plus other sports that they have teams set up in. Stalls and merchandising (the T-shirts and hoodies that I saw were very professional) will be in attendance. Avon Plate have been invited to enter a cricket team. Unfortunately, the football side of the tournament is well organised and has teams from all over the globe taking part. The cricket part has hit snags already and looks tricky to get off the ground but I am hopeful. Of the many fund-raising ideas that were brought up, the possibility of a nude cricket match seems to interest some team members hugely. As usual with the cricket team meetings, huge ideas spring into existence but then cannot be seen through. Although feeling a little guilty, I cannot commit to helping organise anything whilst carrying on my club secretary chores for the Plate.

A lesson was well and truly learnt, one that I should have learnt long before now. When I type 'touch wood' I must actually touch wood as well. Within twenty-four hours of writing that I was injury free (touch wood), and no wood had been touched, my back was giving me some severe grief. The lower back was aching and if I tried to bend over or sit down then there was a sharp pain. By training day I was feeling quite desperate. I had to go to work, as there were important meetings to attend, even though I was walking like a bent old man and occasionally letting out large groans. If I went to work though, I could still try and go to training. As soon as my working day was done I was in a hot bath and stretching out the offending area. For a time this seemed to free up the area and thus I confidently got changed and ready to go to Monks Park. I hid any pain from the wife, as I didn't want her to question the merits of my going to training.

I could not move around enough to break a sweat and running was jarring the old back. My anticipation skills were utilised and developed as there was no way that I could use speed to recover a position or to chase the ball or man. Jumpy and Lee were missing as they also have bad backs, this made me look very committed and tough. It meant that I witnessed yet another training session with twenty plus players. This is too many on a half pitch. It is too easy to close the opposition down; also, you don't get enough touches of the ball. As this has happened for the last three or four weeks, it is time for something to be said to the non-Platers, i.e.: ' Okay lads, as Club Secretary it has been mentioned over the past few weeks that there are too many turning up for this training and the Plate are not getting enough out of it. Unless you are signed onto the Plate, or intend to, we will have to say this is your last training session with us. Any questions?' I am not a great fan of public speaking, especially when some will be upset or whatever, just one more job to do for the club secretary.

Our squad is, seemingly, large enough to cope with the remaining fixtures for this season. Personally, I don't want the non-Platers to join up. However, there are two new blokes to training who should interest the Plate. A friend of Ali's: Nib (great footy name, if indeed that is his moniker) and a mate of Ga, Yos and Sherry: Pob (another cracking footy name). Pob literally wants to play at left back and Nib also seems left-sided. They also both have a degree of talent and fitness. Pob came down the pub after training which is another great sign. He seems keen to join up. Nib I will have to have a word with next week. How we seem to be attracting so many, quality players is beyond me but is absolutely marvellous. Maybe, when our squad was small, we were all mates and a bit insular, it only took a small widening of the circle to capture a whole passive supply of friends-of-friends, newcomers to the area and so on.

My back did actually feel much looser as the night wore on. We sold another old Plate shirt to bring the total raised to £160. This, in combination with what we have over from the Sunday and Thursday Secretaries, should be enough to have an excellent AGM and pay for the rest of the pitch hire plus the odd bits and bobs that I have to pay the league each month. Yos and I went back to his for a session of, 'Medieval Total war'. For the first hour or so we didn't look at the PC. It felt like we had done some Charlie as we talked about the Plate. The squad, the formations, the goals, the hilarity, the spirit, it all made us very excited and eager to take on the league leaders on Sunday. We are in such good form that we even had a decent start a new Total War campaign as the Hungarians.

How time flies, it has been 14 weeks since a proper 'Fantasy league' update. At that point my top team were 63,290th overall and 6th in our 'Super league' with 8 transfers used out of the permitted 30. The game has continued to be incredibly difficult this season. I have had to use all my skills to creep slowly up our super league and mainly just tread water in the overall league. This week I was getting very excited. I knew that the team had earned a shed load of points but when I worked it out there was a total of 116 points. My best ever total in a week. With the kids and all, it wasn't until late in the evening that, with great anticipation I looked at the website. It is week 25 and my top team is now in 35,325th place. Up 10,000 places but still a midge disappointing. In the Super League it was even more of a let down, I remained in third position without catching up more than one solitary point on the leader. Twenty transfers have now been used. The best of the recent bunch has been to bring in Dyer (Newcastle), Taylor (Portsmouth), Rooney (Manchester United) and most usefully Ronaldo (Manchester United). He has played in six of the seven weekends I have had him and has scored an incredible 79 points. It galls me that I had picked out a team which contained the stars who had not performed well (or ended with a point to prove) in the World Cup. Ronaldo being a winker had put him in that team along with the brilliantly scoring Frank Lampard. 'Stick to your guns', 'listen to that little voice in your head' have not become sayings for no good reason.

Sunday 11th February 2007

Brislington 1987 versus Avon Plate

Imperial Ground Bristol & District Sunday League Division 4

As anything other than mild conditions are labelled as 'extreme weather', I suppose we are now entering a new Ice Age as it had the temerity to snow this week. Poor old local news programmes had to try and make this light snowfall appear as a blizzard. When they showed three snowmen in a line, you could tell from the surroundings that every scrap of snow in that vicinity had been used up for the shot. Unfortunately, it snowed and then rained towards the end of the week and therefore, the game is off.

Good news for me as there was no way I could have played a full-on match against the table-toppers with restricted mobility caused by the back pain. Saying that, if the game was on, I would have been in hot baths and stretching and using electric pads throughout the evening in a bid to be fit. How it feels this morning, it might just have worked. It was going to be a big pointer into how far the Plate have really come; could we beat the unbeaten Brislington? Pob was coming to watch and it would have been a tasty introduction for him.

Since I wrote I have no injuries, my back started hurting, when I wrote that my marriage has turned round, we are back to a bit of misery as the wife's iron deficiency has returned to drain her of energy and life force. So, I shall leave these subjects well alone as goodness-knows what will happen. Instead we shall now concentrate on some alternative policies for my imaginary political party that I have been thinking over (usually with self-medicating help).

It is nice to know that some politicians may have concocted some of their policies whilst stoned. Little weasel that he is, at least David Cameron admits to smoking puff when he was younger. His credibility suffers in that he had no choice but to admit it, the incidents were on his school record, and that school was Eton. Still, respect is due, all the other numbskulls in Parliament had, in most cases, a bit of money and a bit of time to kill and would be mixing in the 'Bohemian' circles of the rich and famous' offspring and yet none of them did anything 'naughty' and if they are pushed to recall a joint or two, they didn't inhale. There cannot be too many industries where the protagonists line up to be the most nerdy and weedy. Just goes to show once again that politicians have no idea whatsoever about the society they are supposed to serve. Therefore, in the spirit of scientific experiment, I shall partake in what the politicians fear and see what comes out.

Let's start with something that I have to deal with: council housing, specifically, the annoying properties that stand empty when there is massive demand. How about a system where people have the opportunity to part own these empty houses. The offer would be that someone comes in to a ramshackle property, they do it up to a liveable standard within a certain time period (say three years). In that time they pay no rent as the money they have will be going on maintenance. The council would not pay for or organise the building repairs. Once the three years is up, the property is examined. If the tenant has fulfilled their part of the bargain in creating a habitable and useable home, then they get 50% of the ownership. The proceeds from any sale would be split between the council and the tenant. If the tenant decides to hold onto the property until they die, then the eventual proceeds would be split between the council and the deceased tenant's estate. If, after the initial three years, the property has not been brought up to the required level, the council takes back the property and tries with another tenant. You could start by offering the properties to the highest priority cases and any left would be offered to the rest of those on the councils' rehousing waiting lists.

A favourite of mine that keeps popping into my hazy mind is a 'National Insurance Lottery'. The public loves the Lottery, and the same public dislike tax rises. Thus, if the government needs to raise a couple of billion in funds, they can put a penny or whatever is needed onto income tax. However, a certain percentage of the extra funds will go into a prize fund for a lottery. The computer will pick out a randomly drawn National Insurance number of a working person (who is contributing to the tax rise). The idea would be to create as many millionaires as possible rather than have individual lottery prizes of several million each. It is ridiculous, people will dream that they have an extra £20 at the end of the month, but will then turn their nose up at the lottery until the Euro lottery reaches £100 million. I am not certain of the figures that would be involved but if one pence of income tax raises £2 billion and the government requires £1.5 billion for a project, then £500 million can create 500 millionaires over the period of a year. This would be an incentive to get a job, as only those numbers will be entered for the lottery. There may be an outcry as we seem, as a society, to decry anything that smacks of 'discrimination' or 'difference' but we really should get back into the idea that work is better than benefits.

Am on a roll so rolled another. According to the politicians, I must be near death by now and feeling very foolish. Anyway, next subject is 'Juvenile Behaviour'. The trouble with teenagers is that they want to partake of booze and drugs which are now so common that they aren't considered dangerous, exotic or even that rebellious. However, the youth are too young to go into pubs and clubs so they have to get out of their heads on the streets and in everyone's faces. If adults' drunk and drugged behaviour was in your face, adults would get a bad rap too. The alternatives:

1. Continue current use of prohibition. Especially with the youth, of whatever generation, if they are told, 'Don't take drugs, it is illegal and bad for you' it will not sink in. Whether this advice comes in the guise of, for example, policeman, teacher, counsellor, politician, doctor etc this will not work. It never has and it never will.
2. Leave it to parents and the community. Unfortunately, this idea was scuppered back in the days of Thatcher. It became clear, that in the interests of the middle class, certain communities were 'expendable'. Pretty much anywhere that relied on coal, shipping or steel was okay to be devastated under the rigours of 'Thatcherism'. From then on, a subclass will always have distrust and contempt for authority.
3. Leave it to the legal system. The police are despised by the youth of today. Again, I'm afraid, it goes back to dear old Thatcher. Instead of being an independent crime-fighting force, Thatcher turned them into the government's private army. They were used to brutally crush the resistance to the crushing of the Trades Union movements. Then again used as a hammer against the populace in the anti Poll Tax marches. The police have also been known to be a bastion of racism, corruption, blunders, and a terrible crime-solving rate amongst other things. Short of locking up everyone under the age of eighteen, this is a 'war' that the legal system cannot win.
4. Use education. This must be done in a useful way. How to do drugs safely and not on pointless prohibition tactics.
5. Give the youth a space in which to carry out their desires without it having to be in stairwells, childrens' playgrounds or the streets.

What to do when the behaviour of the future of mankind is then mixed in with gangs, guns and other weaponry? The sure-fire way to break this trend is to legalise recreational drugs.

This, of course, removes the largest and most profitable section of the drug trade: the middlemen. The price of drugs would plummet and thus reduce the crime needed to pay for it. Casual users would not be so exposed to more 'hardened' drug-types and would not be so exposed to some temptations. Gangs would no longer be making the profits required to afford the tools necessary for the mass destruction of each other. Police resources could be deployed to other, more needy, areas of law and order. It would also be safer for the police to walk the streets and actually deter some crime. We would all make money via the taxes from drug sales. These funds could be diverted into proper health provision and education. Mind you, there will be less people in the hospitals because the drugs sold legitimately will be tested and standardised so neither too cut nor too strong for public consumption, people will also be better educated because they can speak more freely. There would be so much extra revenue floating about, most aspects of government could be raised up to a decent standard. General tax cuts could be the way forward for a now rich country like ours.

The prisons would suddenly be half empty and therefore we could actually threaten criminals with justified sentences. The existing resources in the prisons would be ample to rehabilitate the remaining prisoners and their re-offending rate will lessen. This would really be, 'Tough on crime, tough on the causes of crime). Obviously, for one to have this view, one must accept that there is a huge demand for recreational drugs, one that does not appear to be reducing over time, and some elements of society will go to almost any length to get their next score and that the major benefactors of the system are criminal elements which fuels gangs and violence.

Mr Tony Blair set out his one of his key agenda items with the now famous, 'Education, education, education' quote. Little did we know that this was his normal way of speaking, that he hardly ever uses whole sentences as they are not considered catchy enough. It is blindingly obvious that a whole heap of taxpayers' cash has gone into building new schools, renovating others, providing more teachers and equipment such as computers. However, educational standards still appear to be dropping.

Yet again, this problem stems from the great revolution of Thatcher. Her policy of a bastardised version of Adam Smith's Classical Economics and monetarism meant that it was inevitable that as inflation and the unions were conquered, there would be a huge cost in terms of unemployment and social destruction. The masses of unemployed was seen as the only way to cut industries costs and thus reduce prices, killing inflation and making it easier to sell our goods against foreign competition. The unions would have less power as they had fewer members simply as a result of far less people having a job. Sterling would collapse as the economy appeared to be imploding, thus, the pound's value would sink and again our goods would be cheaper and easier to sell, this time in the export market. In order for this to be swallowed by the masses it was necessary to demonise the opposition. Anything remotely socialist was to be attacked and made to look the enemy. The civil Service, Unions, Labour politicians, The BBC were just some of the enemies of Thatcher. She appeared ruthless because she was just that, any other way and her great experiment would have failed. Unfortunately, the lady was not for turning.

The teaching profession was another of these groups targeted by Thatcher. The vast majority of members of such revolutionary (don't make me laugh) organisations as the Socialist Workers Party are dominated by teachers. The education system of pre 1979 was attacked for failing our brightest pupils due to politically correct equal opportunities philosophy. Not enough attention was being put into creating the passive, ignorant, placid robots that were needed for the modern workplace. Teachers promoting fairness and equal chances for all were destroying the entrepreneurial spirit. Teachers, in Thatcher's, 'mind' were not to be trusted and made for a great diversion from scrutiny of what was happening on the rioting streets. It was decided that as teachers could no longer be trusted, it would be up to the politicians to decide how the system would work and be planned. Left in the hands of these rogues and cads, it means that from this point, education was thought of in five year cycles (the length of a parliament) and is therefore subjected to radical upheaval just as they were about to get to grips with the last populist-driven ideas. The abandoning of long-term strategy in favour of short term headlines has been rapidly increasing in its pace until today we have Blair and his scatter-gun quote approach with barely no thought whatsoever to achieving an aim except to survive until the end of his premiership with at least a tiny bit of dignity left. Segregation follows integration, high standards for all is followed by fast-tracking the achievers, a broad curriculum followed by specialisation. Round and round it goes.

Every step of the way, the children and the teachers are tested and examined, assessed, measured and quantified. Because there is no trust, teachers are constantly checked and double-checked. There may be more teachers but there is so much more bureaucracy to justify ones existence. It seems to be the case that our children are now educated to pass tests. There is no time for a broad knowledge and there is no time to learn to think, 'I am told what to achieve and what is a success and I have to blindly follow that, there is no time to stop and stare'. Children are no longer individual bright lights of wonder, they are just another set of statistics, and, as Mr Blair knows well, statistics can be manipulated to show any result you care for. There is no time for extra-curricular activities, there is little or no drama or sport in schools. Teachers are seen as demotivated, boring, narrow-minded and repetitive, and they are under the current system. With so much testing, there is no enjoyment in schooling but there is an abundance of stress. Can't see why there is so much truancy?

Give the teachers some trust back. They are the experts at educating. They can set long-term projects. Removing some of the examinations and testing will give the teaching industry room to breathe and to begin to actually teach once more. Removing these layers of bureaucracy will free up funds to pay for more teachers, reduce class sizes further and provide for even more equipment. The children will be less bored, happier and more fulfilled. They will be fitter and yet more rounded as human beings. It is certainly counter-productive to carry on the way we are, as morale and standards fall, simply make the exams easier and thus the mirage of educational excellence will be maintained. The only people that helps are those like me who can burst a young person's bubble by saying that 'These GCSE's are nothing like the old 'O' level, now there was something worth the paper it was printed on.'

Transport appears to be the casualty in all the spending on education and the war in Iraq, there seems no money left to improve the lot of, especially, our train commuters. It was amusing to see that the solution to the overcrowding was to remove more of the seats to create more space for standing room. Our society and New Labour are very draining. If we could cut the amount we spend on benefits and get people into work that would free up billions. If the amount of crimes were reduced, that would free up vast amounts of money. Stop the war and we wouldn't need to wave goodbye to the £7billion we have reportedly spent so far. If the level of bureaucracy that constituted the 'Nanny State' sections of government were to be removed that would free up money and raise happiness and freedom (who could ask for more?). It seems obvious that if the private companies wont do it, then the government would have to renationalise and simply buy more trains, recruit more staff, introduce safety inspections that have their major concern being for the well being of the passengers rather than the profit and loss column in the financial report.

The natural aid I have been using to help me with developing these ideas has obviously polluted the air somewhat and so my final ravings will concern the environment. How to reach and beat the targets that have been set us all for recycling and to reduce harmful emissions (apart from my negative shouts on a Sunday). At present, we, the public, collect the recycling; we wash it, put it into the correct receptacle, store it, put it out on the correct day onto the street so that the collector doesn't have to walk or carry far. We are then to feel content with having done our bit.

How many industries can there be that get their customers to do so much free work for them? So much of the dirty part of the work too. Recycling should be a multi-billion pound industry. Isn't it time that the public were paid for their efforts?

Of course, closing down all the coal and oil burning power stations would be enormously expensive. As wind and waves are even cheaper than coal, the long term cut in power costs should be an incentive to take this action. The government would also have to raise taxes (use the National Insurance Lottery to soften that blow), to raise taxes and survive, the Prime Minister must have: vision, honesty, strength of character and purpose, morals and not be in it for the money. Only then can someone ride out the short-term storm caused by the dreaded tax rise. Stick to your guns, earn respect, the youth will love you and vote for you as this is an issue closer to their hearts. Cause some real debate and thus get the non-voting majority involved and bothered. As an aside, there is always the satisfaction of saving the bloomin' planet.

All week I have been preparing for the speech to say cheerio to the non-Platers from training. So, of course, there are none of them there. Twelve Platers have made it. As my back is fully recovered, I kicked off training with the intention of running myself into the ground. As I am only thirty-nine years old, I haven't learnt to properly warm up yet and so within a minute, my right knee had turned over with a pistol-crack-type sound.

No pain though so continued as planned. The only other problem came in a tackle with Louis when knee hit my left knee and I immediately felt a sharp pain stab into the side of the kneecap. Adrenalin sorted that out for the duration of the session though.

Having twelve at training meant a tough run around. It is the first time in weeks that we have had this pleasure on a Thursday night. A couple more of these kind of sessions and we will be doing even more damage on A Sunday. Tonight though we were all knackered plus we have no game on Sunday due to us having 'closed' the weekend through the correct channels. It should mean that we have ten games to come with the worst of the winter over.

Sunday 18th February 2007

Avon Plate versus Farmhouse

Frys Club Bristol & District Sunday League Division 4

As previously mentioned, game off due to Avon Plate having 'closed' this weekend off to allow Sherry to go off with some mates for a belated birthday treat.

I was supposed to be earning brownie points a-plenty. The wife was to give an astrology reading Thursday night, attend a group on session on Saturday and then pop to London for an astrological seminar on Sunday. Timing was fabulous for me. My eldest started the ball rolling with a twenty-four hour bug with vomiting and feeling generally crappy. Saturday was my daughter's turn and at about midnight, she stopped vomiting only for Louis to begin his 'sick-shift'. Somehow, I managed to get the house up straight, wash the bedding and floors and clothes, which had been liberally sprinkled, with vomit. The missus will be pleased I thought. It turns out that she had started to show symptoms of the bug on Saturday night too. She hadn't gone to London after all due to feeling so rough. All that bleedin' effort and nothing much for it except that she had the opportunity to be sick in her mum's house rather than her own.

As a final update on my work-related issues, you can add the following to the list: a dispute with a neighbouring drug dealer, family fall-out, benefits appeal process, cyclical behaviour (one relationship to another, usually with kids involved), two emergency re-housing applications, Post Traumatic Stress Disorder, overdosing, moving from supported housing to an independent tenancy, self-harm and an OCD that relates to cleaning and eating behaviours.

The,'caring' government of New Labour are very kindly putting pressure on my lot by continuing to push through funding cuts. They increase the bureaucracy (no bad thing although time-consuming for me and tend to bring up painful issues for the clients), increase the effort we have to put into extra projects such as: new ways of working with our client group ('Recovery' is the current new philosophy on the block), threaten us with wage cuts (awaiting 'consultation' procedure at this time) and to top it off, and certainly the most upsetting is to raise our caseloads and thus reduce our quality and efficiency, but it does make our service cheaper. You must remember that my employers have a fantastic reputation across Bristol and beyond. We are client-orientated, have lots of checks and balances in place, promote and push for better ways of working, keep up with our bureaucracy and do everything that the funders ask of us. Having got to this stage the powers that be would rather we now put all that at risk to 'save' a tiny amount of money. Money that will be spent on increased hospital care and general health bills as people begin to rely on their GPs and taking overdoses and cutting themselves. Money that will also be spent on putting people up in B&Bs as their tenancies fail. Let us hope that money will not instead have to be spent on the jailing of the mentally ill and the costs to those they have damaged whilst ill, frustrated, confused, paranoid, anxious and alone. Go for it Mr Blair, and whilst you are at it, award some more mates of yours an honour, take another holiday that you have 'earned' and for goodness sake give yourself a reasonable pay rise.

As a post script to this section, I have just finished reading the abridged version of Paul McGrath's book: 'Back From The Brink'. A stupendous player, wife, kids, money, success, World Cups, European tournaments, Player of the Year award, a hero in Ireland and elsewhere. Yet here is a man racked by lack of self-worth and that people would 'see through him' at any time. Unfortunately for Paul he was brought up 'in the system' since childhood. As I have mentioned with clients that I work with who have shared the same fate, all are racked by this need to sabotage anything good in their lives and no matter what you tell them, or show them their achievements, they find it nigh on impossible to adjust and take their place in 'normal society'. In Paul's case, as with many others, it is religious groups that take up the mantle of providing orphans and the like with an upbringing. I cannot but help feeling that for religion, insert brutality, meanness, possibly perversion, guilt-galore, prohibitionist and most certainly an unnatural introduction to life.

Training was great on a few levels: There were fifteen players so just about the optimum number, this led to an excellent workout and a good deal of fine form was on show, not least from yours truly. Several of us spent a lovely couple of hours chatting about team selection and personnel. Our newest recruits: Patrick and Pob were both present. We have a large squad available for an important match on Sunday.

Yos and I also conducted an interview with management-hopeful, Sherry. He is of the school of thought that believes strategically placed 'senior players' will command the defence, midfield and attack that would leave the manager with a more straight forward task on a Sunday. He also believes that 'everyone should get a game'. Yos and I put him right on a couple of points. Firstly, there is no delegation of responsibilities; a team like ours (possibly every team) needs to be 'managed' rather than this committee based, 'fairness' policy. Secondly, messing about with the personnel constantly does not make for a winning or happy ship. One thing is for sure, with Jer not showing up for training again, he has lost touch with the squad and I am at a loss to see how much longer he can continue. I usually ring him on the Saturday to confirm the team and give him an update, but, as the talk is of myself going back into centre midfield, I don't see how I can say that without it looking like I am just trying to get myself into the position I want, at training though, it is obvious that a triumvirate of Yos, Dr and myself would be worth a go. Three of the young 'uns would play in front and around us with their speed and trickery and energy whilst with our experience and skills, we can give them the ammunition to fire into the opposition goal. I am not really needed at right back any more as we have Reg, Daz and Jumpy ready to step in there, especially as Pob looks so good and wants to play left back. I actually don't mind playing right back, but I hardly play it in a conventional way, more just an extra midfielder with license to roam. I made a special effort at training tonight to absolutely knacker myself out and try and build some stamina and speed for the rest of the season.

If we are to achieve real success this season (top two finish) then we are going to have to win a lot of games yet. The top two at the moment drew with each other on Sunday and we have Portcullis and our next opponents: South Bristol Wanderers in good form and also pushing for promotion.

On another level, there seemed to be a good deal of personal chat going on which is rare for any group of blokes. Unfortunately, this had to be kick-started with the news that Daz's mother has passed away. He wants to keep training and coming to matches as something of his usual routine that will stop him thinking over and over about his loss. Yos and myself had a long catch up on our histories from before we met and became bosom buddies. That was kicked off by my announcement that I intend to quit all smoking from just after my fortieth birthday at the end of this summer. There is a chance I will be successful as Yos thinks it will be a great idea for me to give up. With his, and the team and family support, and with plenty of reasons for myself to hold onto, I could make it.

Perhaps the only downer on the evening was the bloomin' rain which continues to fall on a far-too-regular basis. Already, we have started to see double fixtures and points being awarded for double fixture matches that aren't being fulfilled. This week, Portcullis benefited with three 'gifted' points as did Oracle. However, Oracle also 'lost / forfeited' three points and Northville were also punished in a similar way. As we have yet to play Oracle this season in the league, we have the joy of a double fixture to come I am sure. As Yos said, ' I would love to play them all day every day'. I second that emotion with the knowledge that I usually score against them too.

Sunday February 25th 2007

South Bristol Wanderers versus Avon Plate

Cutters Club, Stockwood
Bristol & District Sunday League Division 4

As with Mr Tony Blair's policies, the effects of the weather on our league schedule has gone beyond a joke. 'Wank, toss, balls, piss, cock' (Sherry), and ' Arse! Was really looking forward to kicking the shite out of them!' (Daz), sum up the team reaction to the news that yet another game has bitten the mud due to waterlogged pitches. All I can think about is: a) my stamina and 'engine' are not what they once were and this lack of games is thus harming me, b) the strong showing of the squad may not last (if you don't use it you lose it), c) the fixtures may be cocked up so much that we may have to play double fixtures which give false impressions of the season, d) The season may be extended and I will have to spend even more Sundays playing footy and then nipping straight across town for cricket matches, e) I am getting depressed because I am not having my weekly fix of competitive action, and f) the league may decide that teams cannot / do not have to fulfil all their fixtures and the season will just be a write-off as far as a proper contest.

After much gnashing of teeth, the extra day given to us through the match cancellation gave myself and the wife the time to come up with a plan. This involves paying off our debts and giving her the chance to give up her job for a while. The heavy lifting involved has been exacerbating her health problems.

She has now sorted in her head what she wants to do with her future. It appears that part of this is for us to stay together and commit to each other. Both of us have obviously been working on separate plans for the future but now we have discussed them, they do tend to include each other and the family rather than going our separate ways. With love, normally one experiences hormone and endorphin rushes, or the need to orgasm and 'release', or one wants to be close because of an upset or illness or similar. However, recently I have experienced this rather serene desire to be with my wife. It seems to be coming from a very genuine place.

The missus wants me to have a job that I want to do rather than see the job as simply a means to an end, being simply a provider of money for the upkeep of the family. Whether this would be in a management setting within the field of work I am in at the moment, we don't know. Ideally, this book will be published and be a success, in which case I can either retire a rich man or at least become a writer (hopefully on sports related pieces). If not, then I am planning to put together a new CV and try and get into sports administration. Other than that, it looks like the 'caring profession' for the next twenty-five long years. At least they should be years spent within a loving family, with a wife who is so happy and grateful for her caring, sharing husband, that most of those long years will at least be spent in a more intimate, friendly and passionate way.

It may seem that I am rather confused about what exactly is going on in my marriage, and you would be right. Wednesday morning I am being hassled by the wife about my end-of-summer giving up smoking plan. Negative thoughts abound with regards my true intentions of trying to give up the weed and so on. I then receive a text a little later with, 'Am really sorry that I pushed you earlier. I'm beginning to feel like I love you again and that feels risky. I don't want to be hurt again or disappointed.' So, of course, the next morning I lean over for a kiss and she pulls away and states, 'I like you when you aren't here and am not so sure when you are around me'. This may well be the usual, 'absence makes the heart grow fonder' stuff, but she says it just as I am going to work to spend my day with people in various states of depression and desperation. Thus I have the whole day of mulling it over and picking up depressed moods from the clients and so I am mightily confused and pissed off by the time I get home. It is no wonder that the Bronte's and their ilk could churn out romantic novels all the time. It is so confusing and goes around in circles.

Training was again a great workout with an all-Plate showing. Somehow, the non-Platers seem to have got the message that they were not overly welcome. Sixteen showed for a mainly old versus mainly young 'un match. My right knee was again tested to the full. I had to do a tackle on Louis in full flight, my leg was stretched out and we both ended up having about three hacks at the ball. Each hack led to a stretching of the ligaments around my stretched joint. The knee did not explode. A full-on Arnica rub when I got in will hopefully stop any damage for Sunday. At least we worked hard and talked hard about the Plate on the backdrop to a dry day. Up until yesterday (Wednesday) it has been belting down with rain yet again. Today though, sunny and windy so a perfect drying day. I have been emailing the team to sway about, chant and pray for a dry spell. This week would be the last 'good' weekend to have off as we have Ga's fortieth and Dr's thirtieth birthdays to celebrate and they are having the do on the Saturday night, you would think they would be old enough to know better.

Sunday 4th March 2007

Avon Plate versus Longreach Athletic Reserves

Frys Club, Keynesham
Bristol & District Sunday League Division 4
Referee: M Popel (League appointed)

Team:

Sherry
Bolts Patrick Dave Jumpy
Jer
DJ James Korahn Dr Ned
Louis

Substitutes: Reg (for DJ James 30 mins)
Pob (used as ambulance driver)
Ali (unused, linesman)

Next time you hear one of these lazy football commentators say, 'This was a game that had everything', remember this match.

Last night was a very good do for Ga and Dr. Their birthdays were celebrated with some excellent music including the Avon Plate band and The Vistics. Most people got to the venue (Seymours Family Club) at about eight o'clock and nobody left before the place shut for the night. One of our sponsors: The Bristol Beer Factory provided cheap booze that ran out at around midnight but there was still the club's proper bar to hammer. Personally, I had a wicked time. Lots of old chums that were back in Bristol. Lots of chat. We watched a few minutes of the lunar eclipse. I got home at about two thirty but some others went back to Ga's to continue the party. Unfortunately, it meant that we were without Yos and Ga for the game and myself, Jer, Jumpy, Sherry, Reg, Pob, were all feeling distinctly rough as houses.

Pretty much the last thing you want to do with a stinking hangover is go out on a Sunday morning, put shorts on and attempt to run around in the pouring and freezing rain. It is also quite difficult to try and do this on a swamp-like pitch. I had tried to contact Frys in the hope that they would say the game was off but no chance and the referee was quite happy to go for it as well.

With sore heads and missing players (as well as Ga and Yos being out, we had Lee who had worked late last night also unavailable plus Daz was at his mother's funeral and Tyler had a toothache the poor lamb. Tony is still working away) it meant yet another set of changes to the personnel. We still had the necessary fourteen players compared to Longreach who had just the bare eleven.

We kick off in rain being driven by a very cold North wind. The pitch is sodden and the centre circle has a few puddles but the referee is fine with pitch so let's go. The Plate dominates the first half hour. Personally, I have a pretty tasty first quarter of an hour but then begin to tail off quite badly although I can still kick the ball properly, can still head the ball and am not doing anything foolish. We have several shots in that first half hour and are dealing with the conditions rather better, very similar in fact to the last match against Longreach. Fifteen minutes in and I still have it in me to get into the box when Louis has had possession for what seems like a minute or so. After having toyed with three of their defenders out wide, Louis gets in the cross and I get a lovely view of Ned heading in our opening goal.

The Plate young 'uns are driving us on up front. Shot after shot rains in on their 'keeper (the rain itself just keeps keeping on). On one occasion, Korahn outdoes Ronaldo in his step overs and earns us a free kick twenty yards out and central. Jumpy is obviously too hung over and so DJ James steps up. Incredibly, he produces a low curling shot that nestles into the bottom corner of the Longreach net. 2-0 and looking good.

As usual, there is then the usual call for a 'Big ten minutes' of solid play. However, there is a disruption to our plans. DJ James goes into a challenge with their full back and ends up kicking the guy's studs as hard as he can. There seems a loud crack and he goes down immediately and stays down. Eventually, he attempts to run it off but his closeness to tears signals that his match is over. In the still howling wind and rain, he drags himself to the side and is wrapped in many coats. He cannot wait though and gets Pob to drive his car to the pitch to take him to hospital. This will make the grounds staff absolutely furious and they could kick us off the pitch for such an indiscretion. I was playing in the game and didn't really notice what was happening but probably wouldn't have tried to stop him if I had been fully aware. If you have the option of not having to wait for ages for an ambulance, you are getting extremely wet and cold, and are panicking with a possible broken foot, then go for it. After today, the Fry's pitches will hardly be recognisable as such so why worry about a few tyre marks on the non-playing areas. It was at this point he was told that Avon Plate were playing on the wrong pitch and would we swap over to the correct one.

With DJ gone, Jer decides to bring on Reg as a straight swap. I am smiling because with Reg in front of me, that should make my job a whole lot bearable. The problem is that we begin to play badly as a whole. Before half time comes we have conceded a soft goal when Dave is caught out as his man cuts across him at speed and loses him, there is a cross which goes through Patrick and to Jumpy to smash home from about three yards out. There was an opposition player behind him, but still. 2-1. Half time thank goodness.

By now, I am feeling considerably lower than at the start of the match, at which point I was already feeling pretty dull. For the first time I was dreading a second half and just wishing the game was over. Pob must have given Jer the message about the need to change pitch and half the Plate start to troop off. Myself and the other half of the team have no idea what is going on and we don't fancy having to arse about with the poles and checking nets. The referee also seems to be clueless as to the antics so we resume the second half on our original pitch. Looking around, there seemed enough strength and purpose in the rest of the lads to see us through. To give a clue as to my own performance in the first half, even though it was muddy and slippery as hell, my kit was just about clean.

Plate now begins to play badly. Dave is beginning to lose his cool. Everyone agrees he is a top bloke and an uncompromising, old school, no-nonsense centre back. However, he needs to get the balance right between being relaxed, focussed, taking no prisoners and completely mental. With wind and the pitch it has to be said that he and Jumpy look wary of the ball hitting their heads and letting the Longreach long balls bounce leading to a lottery of slides and slices. The ball also manages to go through their legs a couple of times each. In a situation where Plate have two defenders around their player, Dave decides to take him out, thus giving away a free kick on the edge of our box. I try and form a wall, hardly able to concentrate at all. Sherry organises us the best he can. The shot comes in and I manage to just get the outside of my boot to it and think that, as I am on the end of the wall, the ball must surely go out for a corner. Our poor positioning though, means that Sherry ends up palming the ball into the corner of our net. 2-2.

Our defence is now what you would call, amongst other things, hopeless. I am not able to chat to Patrick at all as I am so fuzzy-headed and he is new to the team so could probably do with some help. Dave never really communicates except with the odd rant. Jer and the Dr are struggling to keep going and produce much pretty play in the quagmire centre. Consequently, we have no quality ball to the front three and cannot push up to any great effect. Eventually, I am given the run around by a Longreach attacker (their whole team is growing in confidence as we fall apart) and he runs across Patrick, his heels are clipped, an accident surely? Penalty. 2-3.

Now it does seem a grey old day, playing in this sodding weather with a hangover and not even getting anything out of the game points-wise, awful. Another mazy run from a Longreach attacker sees him being followed by Dave from the half way line, Dave's hands tugging away at the bloke's shirt. I am watching the referee with a steely gaze on what is happening. As they enter our box, they go down, penalty of course. Much gnashing of teeth from the Plate because Dave had let go of him but the ref was waiting to blow at any opportunity. It was this referee that sent Dave off in a cup game against Luckwell earlier in the season, I am not suggesting that this ref is biased against Dave but he obviously doesn't like the more mouthy players. 2-4.

We have now given them an own goal, a deflected free kick, and two penalties. Enough is enough. From the very depths of our Avon Plate inspired pride and soul, we drag ourselves back into the game. We start to play like Avon Plate can. Because I am now trying as hard as I can, but not being in the best state, my kit is no longer clean as I am spending a fair amount of the time on the deck. I am involved in a build up on the right and eventually receive the ball just inside their box. I have the presence of mind to dummy and beat the first defender but am too weary to try the same again and blast the ball at their defender and sail wide. From the resulting corner, Patrick leaps spectacularly, head and knees everywhere and crashes the ball into the net. 3-4.

The belief is back and we have the momentum. There are still a good ten minutes left when a Longreach player hits the turf and doesn't want to get back up. I am thinking how brave he must be to stay laying in the freezing mud when he announces that he has broken his ankle as he heard a snap and it gave way. We wait around for a good fifteen minutes as the ambulance arrives. Three of their team plus the referee carry the injured player to the waiting ambulance (which is not allowed to drive onto the grassy areas). The rest of us are left in the rain and wind for what seemed an age. We couldn't restart because the referee had gone. Eventually I put my rain jacket on and attempted to keep alert. It got to the point where I was running round in very small circles, not wanting to move but knowing I had to for the resumption of the match. Longreach would be down to nine or ten men. The referee wanders back and he comes out with, 'Game abandoned lads, two injuries and the pitch is considered dangerous'. Half of me is delighted that I can go and get showered but part of me is desperately going round the Longreach players to see if they will replay. They seemed keen to finish it but their captain is not as he reckons they will be awarded the result as the match had gone past a certain point. It is their problem that they didn't bring enough players to cover the situation, we have allowed the game to be stopped whilst the injured bloke was dealt with and not had him dragged off the pitch whilst the ambulance arrived, the pitch is in no worse state than at the start, and, although there have been two injuries, they are probably not linked to the state of the pitch.

To top it all off, the changing room showers were set to scalding hot. Completely knackered, dispirited about getting nil point from the game, chilled to the bone and upset at not getting the chance to play the full ninety minutes. I reported the match as abandoned to the league. They will publish the result as 3-4 at this time and will have a look into it as they would with all abandoned matches.

My ghastly day continued in the Greenbank. As my head was muddled, I thought it best to write down some notes of my match report straight away. The part about Dave and Jumpy being scared of the ball had already been written when who should read it but Jumpy. I tried to explain that it said 'scored' but he was not fooled. We seemed to laugh it off but I emailed him when I got home to explain further. Reading my notes is like reading someone's diary, it is always misunderstood and people get hurt. I was putting it in the context of the period where we lost the match. Of course, I know he is not really scared of the ball and I made sure he knew that I was honoured to have served in the trenches for so long with him and he's a lovely geezer and all that jazz. 'No hard feelings', seems to be the response, thank goodness. I could barely drink one pint before heading home, and I was the last to leave the pub except the young 'uns. It was just too hard to be chatty after such a result and day and anti-climax at the end. Such a shame as there had been goals, penalties, shirt of shame moments galore and a good laugh at Sunday morning football in general. One day I hope to look back and just think about that side of things.
Man of the Match: Ned – Goal and graft
Shirt of Shame: Louis – Falling over during the warm up sprint

Much as I would love to simply put this match out of my mind, I have to spend the next couple of days tracking down the pitch manager and grovelling for forgiveness over the driving one of our motors on the grass and using the wrong pitch (one that was used for a Saturday game and should have been protected). 'Luckily', after the constant rain since Saturday night, all the pitches are underwater and so they aren't bothered about us damaging one pitch. With the car, he had already taken into account that the atrocious conditions had led to a mistake being made by us but we were forgiven. I think he appreciated being rung rather than having to chase me. The sad news of the flooded pitches means that already, Sunday's game is hanging by a thread.

Also, I had to compile a report to the league to argue our case for a replay of the match rather than awarding the result to Longreach just because a certain amount of time had been played. The argument runs thusly: Firstly, we allowed play to be stopped for a good twenty minutes whilst the ambulance was called, we could have insisted that the guy was taken off the pitch and the game resumed. Secondly, we then allowed the guy to be taken off to the ambulance and play stopped for another twenty minutes or so, again we could have insisted the guy was taken and the match resumed as soon as possible. Therefore, it was because we allowed their player to be looked after, that we could now be faced with losing the game. We shall see.

In the Telegraph's Fantasy League, it is no surprise to learn that in the, 'celebrity battle' between Alan Hansen and Richard Branson, Hansen has just gone into the lead. This can possibly be attributed to Branson no longer having access to Sky Sports News. Since Virgin took over ntl:Telewest, Sky has withdrawn the Sky One, Sky News and Sky Sports News channels. I didn't realise quite how much I watched the Sports News channel until it was taken from me. If it was financially viable, and wasn't such a pain in the arse to switch TV, phone and broadband provider I would. Not a good show that Virgin take over and their customer service now sucks, they aren't providing three of the main channels they are supposed to, and, according to sources close to me, have said that the reception since the switch has gone down in standard. Back to the Fantasy League and my own team has scored over the average points for the last six weeks, it has risen to the dizzy heights of 22,579th and is a very close second in the work super league.

Another team in Second place are the mighty Rams. After a 'crisis' reported in the press, which consisted of two whole league defeats in a row, Derby have got back on track with wins over Colchester (5-1 at home) and Norwich (2-1 away) but were halted by losing away 1-0 at Birmingham on their disgrace of a pitch. We have yet to hear about any punishment due to Brum for cancelling the match against Leicester at the last moment because they couldn't lay the thing in time and then have laid the piece of nonsense that is there now. If Birmingham go up, it will be like Oldham, Luton and QPR getting success off the back of their plastic pitches. Once they are in the Prem, Birmingham will find out, again, that they cannot get away with 'cheating' like this and they will be relegated forthwith. Unfortunately, they may have deprived a team that really deserves the promotion place.

I could possibly teach the Birmingham club secretary a lesson. They cannot seem to provide a decent playing surface or fulfil their fixtures but I have to. Due to the winter downpour, even Plate have a double fixture to arrange. Also, with Bristol Rovers in the glamorous paint-pot final on Sunday 1st April, Portcullis are trying to rearrange the fixture as they have some players going. It is either play them in an afternoon match on Easter Sunday or 15th April, or make them play with what they have got. I will check with the team this Sunday and wonder what we shall choose?

If Birmingham City are finding it difficult to run a proper operation, thank the Lord that they are not in charge of the war in Iraq. It seems to be run badly enough already thank you. I would love to give an informed update on the current situation. However, one day we read that the allies are doing well and it is nearly over, the South is cleared up now, the provisional government is about to take full control and arrange proper elections (i.e. NOT like a George W Bush, and his brother, election) but the next day we see that the troops are on their last legs, they are out of supplies and reinforcements.
The very latest developments seem to involve the US talking to the Iranian and Syrian governments in order to enlist their help in calming down Iraq. On the one hand, this could be viewed as a brave step. It should be applauded as a move towards a more long-lasting, stable peace in the region. On the other hand, Iraq and Syria have been called the 'Axis of Evil' when it comes to

exporting terrorism and anti-American feeling. Was a war worth fighting to get rid of Saddam only to replace him with other anti-Western regimes that are certainly more involved in terrorism than Saddam was?

In Afghanistan, the numbers of British, US and other forces totals a less-than-whopping 5,500 troops. How are we supposed to be fighting a war, taking prisoners, guarding our rear, rounding up terrorists, searching the mountains for Al Q'eeda training camps, keeping the Taliban at bay and allowing the country to reconstruct? Perhaps we shall see some good news and even 'victory' just as that nice Mr Blair leaves office.

Training was another top workout, sixteen players again showed. Jer is beginning to get his timing back and has started to win some of his trademark shoulder barges. The Dr and Ga continue to look the worse-for-wear after a week of birthday celebrations and of living together in Si's house now that the Plate centre back has moved to Cornwall for a while. Daz needs to get back up to speed following a traumatic time. However, in general, the size and quality of the squad, plus its team spirit, remains healthy.

A bit of a conundrum now though. Jer is going to be away and thus Yos is going to pick the squad. I had awoken this morning feeling quite upset at being a right back. I was desperate to play in centre midfield. All those goals I was missing out on, watching novices like Ga and Jer mucking about in there, in my position. Back to Yos' and I'm pretty sure that I had convinced him to pick myself for the centre with Reg in as right back. I have some misgivings though. Firstly, it will be obvious that I have used my influence and players like Reg and Ga want to play there. Reg is probably the right sort and so I feel a little guilty about stepping in front of him. Ga could be fine there but it is late in his career to come along and be first choice in that position. Also, I have to think of my long-term place. What if I am rubbish on Sunday, I'm not that unhappy at right back to give up that starting position to be a substitute midfielder. At this level, just being such a regular a match-attendee would probably get me my place back at some point but you never know.

Sunday 11th March 2007

Avon Plate versus Oracle

Frys Club, Keynesham
Bristol & District Sunday League Division 4
Referee: G Miles

Team:

	Sherry		
Reg	Patrick	Dave	Jumpy
Ga	Bolts	Yos	Ned
	Korahn	Louis	

Substitutes: Pob (for Ga at half time)
Daz (unused, linesman)

Pulling into Frys, one couldn't help but marvel at the new natural wonder. There was a lake that covered the pitch we played on last week plus the surrounding pitches too. Thankfully, apart from the bottom pitches, there were three or four others and it is pitch six which would host today's attempt at football glory for the Plate. This lake exists even though we have three whole days without rain. Today is a dry and only slightly windy day, certainly feels like spring, no frost even after a clear night.

My being pushed into centre midfield became less of a choice once we had found out that the Dr had gone for a night out in Cornwall and then ended up stranded in Exeter overnight.

Typical of the Dr, on the pitch you can rely on him, but do so at your peril off the pitch. I couldn't help but cheer when Platers arrived and I was almost dancing round the changing room. Such a good mood has been promoted by the fact we are no longer in the hunt to be promoted unless something dramatic happens. Pressure is off, the monsoon is hopefully over and Plate look healthy in numbers and talent.

I cannot remember a time when I have last spent an hour and a half of such frustration. Probably the last time was as a sex-starved teenager. You know how it goes, you beg for sex all night, every night for months, one evening, you decide not to push it and of course then the girl will turn round and say, 'Oh I really wanted it last night, if only you'd asked'. Thankfully, the frustration of today wasn't matched with an ache in the groin.

This match was a clash of two styles. Throughout the game, Plate kept on trying to play the game with the ball on the floor, movement, organisation and hard work. The ground was as bobbly as heck. Thus, we created many half chances and had tons of possession in and around their box, but the ball just wouldn't fall kindly or sit up for the shot. There were, therefore, groans a-plenty as the ball sailed over and wide, or the final ball was inches away from being a really telling one. On the other hand, you have Oracle. They took the 'long ball' philosophy to its absolute extreme. Every single time they got the ball, no matter whereabouts on the pitch they were, the Oracle players would whack it as high and long as they could. What a day to be in the centre. One second I am involved in a Plate build-up and the next I am hurtling back as they hoof yet another clearance anywhere towards our goal. If it wasn't a long ball, it was a long throw instead. It is a skill that is not seen too much in the Sunday Leagues. None of our lot can throw it any distance without it being called a foul-throw. The Oracle chap can launch them into the back post area from anywhere inside the opposition half. Boring to play against and must be even more boring to play that way every week. Personally, I cannot see the reason for playing football if one has no motivation to improve. At least the Oracle boys have not got a, 'nasty' side to them.

The first half was relatively easy. The slight wind was in our favour and their long whacks were being held up outside of our box and easy meat for Patrick and Yos with myself looking on in admiration. Once we had seen a couple of the long throws, we soon had everyone packed onto our far post to counter them. Deservedly, Plate went 1-0 up. A corner was headed on by Patrick, it went beyond the far post but Ned chased this lost-cause and managed to pull it back, straight onto Yos' left foot and into the back of the net. No matter how much we dominated possession, you cannot have total control of a team that can get the ball from one box to the other in a matter of a couple of seconds. On one occasion we had to concede a corner and the result was a totally free header for their chap who duly made it 1-1.

We kept at them but our front three were making the wrong choices too often. When players like myself were busting a gut to join them in attack, they would play it amongst themselves and either lose possession or waste another shooting opportunity. When they didn't have support they would then choose to try and bring other players into it and so lose possession. Finally, just before half time, some of their 'pitter patter' football paid off; a lovely one-two between Louis and Korahn saw the aforementioned striker crack a lovely finish into the roof of the net.

There was absolutely no change whatsoever in the second half. Pass, pass, ooh close, hoof, scramble. The tactics may not have changed but the referee seemed to. Suddenly, most Plate throws were being called as foul. Blatant saves by the Oracle keeper were going out but being given as goal kicks. He had a word with myself for swearing and others were similarly threatened for daring to open their mouths even if they were swearing at themselves. It is quite nice to have a Sunday referee who is a real stickler for detail, no jewellery, no swearing, throws and kicks from the exact millimetre, but this guy was a bit much especially as everything was going Oracle's way.

At one point in the second half, we were struggling to clear the ball. With the wind now against us, we gave away a series of throw ins in our own half. Usually, we would have a couple of throw ins and gradually got up the field and got some decent ball. This time though, the long-throw merchant could chuck the ball into dangerous area for minutes on end. Eventually, there was a throw, a scramble and a messy goal. 2-2. For the rest of the match we pressed and harried and threatened their goal on a huge number of occasions but their 'keeper had a storming game and their goal lived a charmed life. The referee made certain he would not be seen as popular in our neck of the woods; as we attacked down our left, the cross just about to come in, the ref blows for full time. 'No way' etc etc but that's footy so there are handshakes all round and a lot of smiles from the Oracle team.

Although the game is over, the referee sends off Sherry after he uttered, 'Ref, you are a cheating bastard wanker'. This leads to one of the funniest and, at some levels, disturbing incidents of the season. We have trooped into the changing room and Yos (manager for the day) is rowing with Sherry for his stupid outburst. When things are not resolved to his liking, Yos boots a table in a stunning recreation of his earlier volley. Must have been how the Beckham / Sir Alex incident arose with the flying boot in the eye. It takes Yos all of five minutes to calm down but it is rather wonderful for such emotion to be shown. All a bit of an eye opener for Pob. His first match last week ended up with him taking DJ James to the hospital and this week he makes his debut and witnesses a rare Plate fall-out. His actual play did not live up to what we have seen on a Thursday night at training. Eleven-a-side, on grass, with opposition is a unique experience but I am sure he will soon get to the pace of the game and excel.

The referee grabbed me in the car park afterwards and said that if Sherry rang him before 6pm, and apologised, he would not report the sending off. The most important issue for the club is that Sherry would be banned for at least one game. He is our only goalkeeper. He would save himself some money too (about £30). He was adamant that he would not back down. Plate took it in turns to try and persuade him otherwise but pride did indeed fuck with his head.

We thought we had better put on a show of buying a round at the Frys Club bar, after last week's transgressions. By the time we got to the Greenbank, both of my shins felt like they had barbwire bracelets around them. As reported earlier, the ground was very bobbly today, thus, there were instances where the ball would have been but instead, the stud of an opposition player's boot would gouge into my legs. One of them has a gorgeous drag-scrape leading away from the stud hole. I would very much like to see a Tarantino-esque film in which there is the usual guns and knives carnage. However, one of the tough guys will get a splinter, or catch a hangnail, or perhaps bump a grazed elbow and the guy would reel in agony. This is after him having been shot and stabbed a dozen or so times.
Man of the Match: Patrick – dealing with their long ball 'threat'
Shirt of Shame: Obviously Sherry for the sending off offence, made even worse by him giving a pre-match talk about the referee being good, but not being tolerant on swearing.

Training was acceptable in that we had a knock around. We had the worst number though, eleven, so no even sides and a lot of running around needed. Alas, I was on the team with five players. The standard of Plate play was not of the highest quality either.

Not much in this modern world is what you would call efficient. However, you can leave the GFA (Gloucestershire Football Association) out of this as I have already received the documentation regarding Sherry's weekend sending off. Incredibly, he will be hit with a £33 fine and a 35-day ban which would take in the 9th April to 6th of May and then continue from3rd September to 9th September. He can appeal for leniency but that will cost him another £8 with no guarantee of success. A real dilemma for the Plate though, Sherry is the only 'keeper on our books.

Sunday 18th March 2007

R & P Wonderboys versus Avon Plate

Canford Park Bristol & District Sunday League Division 4

Team:

Sherry

Bolts Reg Jer Jumpy

Dr

Ga Korahn Yos Ned

Louis

Substitutes: Pob (for Ga 70mins)

Referee: No league appointed referee

An early start as usual. This Sunday though is Mothers Day. Prior to shooting off to the footy I have to organise the presents and cards that the twins have been making this past week. I can set off to meet up with the Plate with a warm glow; the plants I bought for my wife have gone down very well. I even remembered to send a card to my own mother.

No guilty conscience but I feel extremely fatigued. I am no hero but the extra bit I have to do, whilst the wife is ill with a serious chest infection, is taking its toll, plus busy at work, the three kids, and the cricket world cup being on late at night. As it is in the West Indies I feel it only right to have a smoke or three before the matches are shown. I was hoping to learn something about batting during this tournament. So far the openers have really struggled and the rest are just whacking it out of the ground or getting out. Only England are playing in the old style: build a solid foundation and go a bit nuts at the death with wickets in hand. It has been a strange old World Cup so far, Pakistan out after losing to the Windies and Ireland, Pakistan lost to Bangladesh and the minnows of England managed to turn over the Canadians. Bob Woolmer has died today. There has also been a ridiculous furore about Freddie Flintoff being out late at night on a pedalo. When one reads most autobiographies by top sports stars, you notice a trend. That the 'maverick' types, the 'flair' players, tend to resist being ordered around, hate being asked to behave like a 'robot', and detest being penned inside a training camp environment. Every time England travel away for any period, there will usually be an incident like this Flintoff one. If we want these gifted and unusual individuals to represent us, then we have to take what goes with that. Yes, we should ensure that talent is not wasted to alcoholism or gambling addiction and so on, but one cannot stifle creativity or it ceases to be creative. What I find particularly annoying are the newspapers. After the Ashes triumph in '95, they hailed Flintoff et al as heroes and 'great blokes' for their obvious partying and boozing ways. Now, those same papers have loads of World Cup column inches to fill and so they make a mountain out of any molehill they can find / invent.

Out of the door to find that winter is having its last fling. Overnight rain has been followed by a cold and howling wind. Plate have only twelve on show. Unfortunately, Tyler has failed to get out of bed and will miss another chance to stake his place in the squad. Still, we have a good team out. A shirt of shame moment as Ga realises that he has forgotten the kit and will have to be driven home and back by Pob to collect it. Not the best preparation although it is better to be inside the changing room that 'warming up' out in the gale. One of their blokes has to referee. Thankfully, there is none of the destructive pre-game chat that was occurring in the early part of the season. I wouldn't have been surprised if one or two hadn't mentioned the ref and the cold and the bobbly pitch (for it certainly was), but everyone seemed up for it.

Plate had the wind for the first half and it was a big advantage, goal kicks were bending back on themselves, clearances very difficult, and for us it was easy to turn defence into attack within a few seconds. The opening forty-five was just as frustrating as last week. We created opportunity after another. Corners, crosses and shots rained in. In all areas of the pitch, we dominated. The whole lot of us were working hard and playing some decent stuff. The young 'uns had the beating of their men and the Dr and Yos were fighting hard in the centre. Sherry had no saves to make in this period. Approximately thirty-five minutes into the half and the referee decides to use his power to end the battering a little early. It wouldn't have seemed quite so obvious but ten minutes (at least) short is a long time and the game on the next pitch kicked off at the same time and was still playing throughout our half time break.

At this point I am privately seething at our profligacy in front of goal, again. All I can see is R & P having the favourable wind and scoring a scrappy goal or two to show our flair players how it should be done. I can also look forward to three quarters of an hour of running backwards as they launch the ball into the wind so if I try and attack I am going to be out of position and knackered. Still, at least we have extra energy to defend, as we have not been playing for very long.

My worst fears seem to come true almost straight away. After a twenty-yard or so battle, Jer manages to push his opposition player out wide in the box, into a position where he cannot score. However, Jer decides to dive in at their bloke and bring him down. The resultant penalty is dispatched and Plate are 1-0 down, about three minutes into the half. I am afraid that an amount of expletives did issue forth from my mouth but I was gripped by a mood that no matter what, if I can change this with effort and a bit of balls then I will. The way we play as a team from then on, it must be a common thought amongst us.

For a while, we struggle but eventually get to grips with the wind. Our game is mainly played on the floor anyway, so it suits us more than them. At the back we are quite manly. We do not let the ball bounce and are heading and clearing with gusto. The conditions are suiting the young 'uns as we are forced to play decent ball to them, instead of long balls into the channels, and they can then make hay. On fifty-six minutes, some of our good play reaps a reward. Jumpy plays a 1-2 with Dr and then a lovely through ball to Ga, he nearly stumbles and messes it up but manages to knock it back to Korahn who puts it into the top left corner. 1-1. The R & P captain had gone down with injury during the move and he was furious that we hadn't kicked the ball out of play. Obviously, he wasn't aware that the laws of the game had been changed so that teams do not have to kick the ball out in this circumstance. Plus, the ball had gone a long way, very quickly, from where he went down, the scorer had no idea that man was down, and he wasn't even injured. After a bit of moaning, the game seems to settle down again.

We manage a solid five minutes before the Wonderboys are awarded a free kick on the edge of our box. Sherry manages to parry their shot but it falls to one of their fast-reacting players to head in. 1-2. I feel completely done in. Pob has come on for Ga and we have no more substitutes. As it turns out, the first half had been taken so easy, that I was just getting my second wind when I usually get it after the first ten minutes or so.

In exemplary fashion, Plate carry on carrying on. The back five solid, Dr messing up their play, Yos all over the shop, Jumpy is enjoying having moved to right midfield after Pob takes over at left back, the young 'uns playing high energy football. There then comes a moment that I will try and forget or at least put to the back of my mind, I am having terrible trouble doing so at the moment though. I was pushing further up the pitch as we again began to turn the screw. I received the ball just outside their box, shifted it to my left foot and hit a low beauty that crept into the bottom corner. Just as it was about to go in, Korahn appeared and I thought 'Don't you dare get a touch on that', however, although not touching it, the damage was done as the goal was disallowed for him being offside and interfering with play. There was the feeling of just being glad to know that I can still score, but I was gutted to the core.

Just a few minutes later and the pain is somewhat dulled when Jumpy plays a ball forward to Louis who holds off the defender, knocks the ball to Korahn whilst continuing to sneakily hold on to the defender and thus Korahn has an almost open goal in which to equalise. 2-2. It is weird, the Plate around me are going nuts but for some reason I cannot share the excitement, this is a hard match and there is a danger that if we take our foot off the gas for a moment, we will be punished and we don't want to be feeling crappy in the pub again.

With the equalizer comes a change in the game. The Wonderboys captain loses his cool. At one point he throws punches at Korahn after a foul and is held onto by Dr as he tries to get at Yos. Their no.7 is also going for it. This is their centre midfield pairing and they decide to hack down anything that comes their way. The air is turned blue through their desperate sounding language. Whenever we try to build through the centre there is the loud crack of a shin being kicked and a Plate player flying through the air. Unfortunately, the referee's whistle is being heard less often as the game begins to get out of control. In this atmosphere,Yos attempts an outrageous dive as he leaps into the air just before a tackle which then sends him flying. The Plate respond by playing to whatever whistle there is, we give as good as we get in the tackles and we continue to play football and doing the right things: we keep on pressing them, we pass our way out of trouble, we remain solid at the back. The other nine players for R & P seem equally embarrassed by the behaviour of 4 and 7 but all of them appear to be running on empty. Plate now dominate the rest of the match and on eighty minutes Louis scores after dribbling round his man and finishing clinically. 3-2 to the Plate. Even though this half is much longer than the first, the whistle does eventually go for full time.

We cannot underestimate the importance of this very fine win. Plate will usually lose, or have abandoned, or feel robbed, when we play a game like this. We usually do not cope well with: teams that are physically aggressive towards us; this type of weather (especially when we hadn't taken any advantage in the first half); a referee from the other teams who loses control and could be called biased, and going behind twice. There is now no need to fear any situation ever again. Finally, we can see that by just keeping playing the game as it should be played, we can be victorious. No more will we turn up to a match with trepidation about anything other than the talent of the opposition. We should not be able to beat ourselves before we step onto the pitch and we should be able to cope with the sort of situations that a Sunday morning football match can throw up. We are strong in spirit and physically capable of looking after ourselves. We are not a half bad football team either. Makes ya proud.

The chat in the pub was obviously of a very positive nature. Not only the performance but also the landlord had food ready for us when we turned up.
Man of the Match: Korahn – it was his birthday (19!)
Shirt of Shame: Ga – forgetting the kit (although Korahn got a mention for getting my goal disallowed, the mention did come from myself).

Training was enjoyable even though we had thirteen players and thus an odd number to split between the teams. There was a lot of quality on show and the chance to relive the weekend's greatness. I managed to charge round like a good 'un and my engine seems to be recovering. Watch out Farmhouse on Sunday.

After the pub, Yos and I went back to his to watch some cricket. We warmed up with a couple of hours of highlights from the England victory in the last Ashes tour over here and settled down for the Dutch versus Scotland game. The Scots were so poor it made one want to boo and trot out the old, 'Scotland never make it past the first round of any World Cup'. We were not bored with the World Cup for long though. We sat stunned whilst the telly-box told us that Bob Woolmer had been murdered. Manual strangulation. It hardly seems credible to think of that gentle and popular man being killed over cricket. This has all happened after the Irish had beaten, and knocked out, Pakistan. The only plausible explanation must be that someone has lost a shed load of money with Pakistan going out and they have taken out their rage on Mr Woolmer or, as the Pakistan region seems to gamble rather heavily on sporting matches, the murderer would be involved with betting-ring gangs.

It puts the bloomin' furore over Flintoff having a few drinks late at night into perspective. Throughout sporting history, the maverick players, the flair players, the 'loose cannons', have railed against their employers and the regimes imposed on them. These large-than-life characters need to express themselves on and off the field of play. Many people will respond well to team bonding, dressing the same, eating and playing together, training every possible moment and so on. Others will respond badly to it. In my era we had Botham, Gower, Tuffnell etc who were loved and then pounced on by the media for their over exuberances. Oh for the days when there were only a small handful of journalists on location, reports were filed concerning the actual game, and players, journalists and fans all mixing and enjoying their glamorous and exciting lives. Nowadays, each is wary of the other and all want different things. The players want to win a tournament. The press need sensation and characters (character assassinations more likely). The fans are squeezed for every spare penny and so they impatient and likely to turn on players. They are confused and confusing. They want success straight away, but also to plan for the future. They want their sporting heroes to be approachable and 'one of us' but if this happens there is moral outrage. If only the BBC would concentrate on the play rather than on side issues, I may actually learn something about batting during this tournament.

Sunday 25th March 2007

Avon Plate versus Farmhouse

Frys Club, Keynesham Bristol & District Sunday League Division 4

Team:

Sherry

Bolts Reg Jer Jumpy

Dr

Tyler Yos Korahn Ned

Louis

Substitutes: None

Referee: T Wren (league appointed)

The bi-annual thorn in Sunday league football struck today. The clocks went forward last night / this morning, an hours sleep is gone, and who will it catch out? Ned is woken by myself when I call to pick him up. The Dr was, of course, caught out. Jumpy (who had the flag poles to mark out the pitch) arrived just on kick off time. At least we now had a proper pitch and eleven men to put out.

Pob has gone missing. Lee is still out with a bad back. Dave is working. Daz is in Nottingham. Patrick is in Brazil.Ga is in Derby. DJ James is still injured. It appears that Ali has had enough. It was lucky that I had contacted Tyler to make a special effort to get along as he would definitely get a run out, turns out he gets a full ninety. Although there is a proper ref, we have no linesman and no substitutes. Farmhouse has a full compliment. For the first time in a while we have a flat and carpet-like pitch. A bit of a wind blowing across the ground but nothing compared to the last couple of weeks.

Kick off and I am involved straight away, my attempted pass into the right channel is straight and true and miles long, must get used to the fact this pitch is running true and smooth. Within two minutes and I have my first shot when I jink inside their defender, onto my left foot and as I am about to let fly my boots go from under me on the slick turf and my shot is tame and easily saved. Still, a good sign that already myself and Tyler have the right hand side under wraps. We have already created a few decent chances when a penalty is awarded. Unfortunately, it goes to Farmhouse. The referee is verbally abused but it looked like a pen to me and it is so bloomin' stupid to keep doing this; again, our defender (the Dr this time) forces the opposition into the corner into a non-scoring area and then brings down the player. All that friendly chat I had with the ref before the game obviously cut no ice. Thankfully, this time we are reprieved as their bloke hits a daisy cutter straight at the grateful Sherry. A let-off which we are determined not to happen again. We experience a few minutes where we are shouting at each other as we attempt to properly organise ourselves.

From then on, the only threat to a great day out for the Plate is the growing frustration. Chance after chance goes begging. It is a replica of last week's first half, all the possession and chances but nothing to show for it on the score sheet. The fear is that we will end up blowing another three points and the young 'uns attack would have to be relooked at. Yos ends up having a quiet go at me and I must agree that even though we are blowing chances galore, it is fantastic to be involved in the Plate on a day like this. Some of the passing and movement is sensational.

The discipline and shape of the team is exceptional, the work rate first class and when we have to play it ugly, we do that with aplomb. However, one of the few pressure moments produces a shirt of shame moment par excellence. A long ball from Farmhouse bounces just in our half and, with Jer shielding the ball, goes right through for a Plate goal kick. Sherry and Jer start to have a heated debate concerning Sherry's inability to come off his line and claim the ball. In a fit of pique, Jer hammers the ball at Sherry. Unfortunately, his aim is straight and true and straight between Sherry's eyes, putting him on the floor for a couple of minutes. The rest of us saw the funny side.

For the remainder of the first period, it is Plate all the way. Wave upon wave of attacks are launched, many shots go just wide, their goalie has a brilliant game and other Plate moves break down after faffing about on the edge of their box. In retaliation, Farmhouse are unable to mount any challenge. On the half hour our reward finally comes. As usual, Plate won the second-ball, Louis who slotted the ball through to Tyler. Considering the amount of chances already, Tyler steadies himself before a calm and clinical finish to their 'keeper's left. 1-0 at last and the frustration is eased, as the déjà vu spell is broken.

Half time does see a sort of team talk, just a, 'Keep it going lads but with even more effort and confidence.' The rest of the interval is spent enjoying Tyler's half time vomiting show. He is not the first Plater to play their first full match, score and be sick. His brother: Korahn experienced it and Louis too this very season.

Back to it for the second half. If there is an advantage from the wind, we now have it. Plate pick up where we left off. Absolutely dominant. Apart from a couple of corners (a header hits our bar) and a free kick that Sherry punches away in continental style, they have nothing in the footballing stakes. Within five minutes of the restart, it is 2-0 to the Plate. Louis is played the ball, he flicked it onto Tyler for a first time ball through to Korahn who attempted a chip but the ball hit the onrushing 'keeper and looped high into the air, it bounced on the line and went in. Now we have the breathing space of a two-goal lead, we can totally relax and let the footy flow.

As is fairly usual on a Sunday morning, once a team is really up against it, they resort to violence. Farmhouse are being dicked by liquid football and some of them cannot handle it. There is the almost constant sound of stud on Plate shin pad. Sneaky punches are thrown into midriffs. The ref is getting a good old shouting-at as he has to keep blowing for fouls against farmhouse. A piece of déjà vu that was most welcome was that we kept on playing under the barrage. A long kick from Sherry's hands catches the wind and bounces deep into the farmhouse half. Louis lets it carry on bouncing into the penalty area, their 'keeper stayed on the line so a left foot tap in was all that was needed to make it 3-0 to the Plate.

A typical moment of the rest of the game came when I was brutally studded on the inner left thigh, a few centimetres from my crown jewels. I had to go down and their number 3 was calling me a 'diving cheat' and when I said something witty back, I was apparently, ' a fucking prick'. Their centre midfield was no longer involved in the actual game. They were simply there to hack but they were too slow and not good enough to catch us.

Some of the stuff we played now was exquisite. The goals did not dry up either. A Jumpy corner was met by Korahn before their 'keeper could claim it, 4-0. A ball was played from Bolts to Tyler who skipped past his man and crossed, Yos went up with the 'keeper and defender so the ball went through to Louis out wide of the box, he 'dicked' his marker and smashed in a shot from an acute angle.

Still we didn't let up. Their number 3 was finally yellow carded for a tackle that was so late, that Ned had received the ball and shot before it happened. Two minutes later, and the bloke was sent off for swearing at the ref. It seemed to be the ever popular, 'Cheating bastard' type of affair. Soon afterwards, the ref brought an end to Farmhouses' pain with the final whistle. 5-0. Handshakes all round as it must have been difficult to play ninety minutes without any dominance or much possession.

A main topic of discussion revolves around the perhaps unique event of keeping two clean sheets against the same team in the same season. All of us that have been part of the Plate for the whole ten years agreed that this was the first time. It feels professional and exceedingly manly. There are sandwiches prepared for our arrival, which also provokes favourable discussion. With food and the fabulous staff, we are really settling well into the Greenbank. Also, we are very pleased with having come through another physical challenge and risen to it. We have at least one more test that will be stern in this manner, the return match against Northville. It feels like we are ready for it now. Finally, we have won this time without a linesman, against a team whose main tactic was to go long ball, this is an achievement. After last week seemingly one of our best wins ever for what we overcame, this week ranks right up there as it was so enjoyable and so dominant.
Man of the Match: Tyler – great debut and goal
Shirt of Shame: Jer – for the obvious 'smack head' moment. (Thus Tyler gets away with being copiously sick and Jumpy gets away with being late)

The story that has caught my eye this week concerns the anniversary of the abolition of slavery in this country. Should we, as a nation, say sorry for our part in the trade? Should we somehow pay reparation monies to compensate, as we did the slave owners with a £20million one-off bonanza (I think I read that this was the equivalent of £2billion today)? My view is yes to the first and no to the second of these questions. The period of history, during which the slave trade flourished, had also created Social Darwinism. This idea was put forward and developed by the intellectuals and philosophers of the day and was espoused by the ruling class as one of the means to justify slavery. Also, the Church of England used slaves and was given monetary compensation when slavery was abolished. Thus, the idea was enshrined in those that could be seemingly trusted. As our society matured, slavery was ended, without the need of a civil war as in the States. So, yes, we are sorry when we look back, but it just seemed like another fact of life in those days and not an evil thing to do.

It is similar to the Japanese not wanting to say sorry for their actions in World War Two. Some of their actions were reprehensible in our eyes. However, at the time, the Japanese did believe their Emperor was an Earth-bound God. They also believed that that they were superior as a race. They believed in, 'Victory at all costs' so much, that some became kamikaze pilots and soldiers. You can't really say sorry for doing something you believed was right.

Will the West soon be saying sorry because we were fully aware that 30,000 children were dying every day when we have plenty of money and food for all? No, of course not. We believe in the system.

Do you see Thatcher saying sorry for crushing any sort of enjoyment out of so many communities, for turning the village bobby into a thug of the government used to silence any meaningful dissent, for helping to destroy socialism and the last capitalist chance of a decent and more just life for the majority, for taking the decision that poor people only suffered because the welfare state and the unions had spoilt them so much. No, she doesn't say sorry and nor should she, she believed in what she was doing, although the way she used brute force to crush opposition is harder to pardon.

It breaks your heart to see one of Thatcher's heroes: Adam Smith appearing on the brand new £20 note. We have come to revere someone who witnessed the economic miracle of power and money in the hands of the few with the masses living in slum conditions and called it a success. We may as well put a slave trader on the note instead, a philosophy equally justified and yet immoral.

I may have been a tad critical of Mr Tony Blair's government, but where I live, we are witnessing almost 'Old Labour' actions by the state and the council. Thatcher wanted council tenants to buy their properties, and not replace the stock, because it was believed that without ownership of their home, the tenants did not look after the property, it falls into disrepair and the community goes downhill. No thought that it could be the failed Modernist housing experiments that had gone horribly wrong, or that the estates were in disrepair because the country had been skint for years and badly managed since way back. Well, round my way, since we moved here roughly three years ago, a school and leisure centre have been built and every single council house has had work carried out. New fascias, insulation and complete refurbishments of blocks of flats have occurred. Our neighbours are council tenants, they had a rotting sofa in the back garden, it was all overgrown out there and at the front. Since the work has been carried out, the sofa is gone, their garden is trimmed, their car is even cleaner. My belief being that if you give people the impression that society gives a damn, and provide something to be proud of in the first place, then a community can flourish. I wish it were a simple Socialist sentiment that was driving this. However, I do believe that Barratt Homes are going to build a fair amount of new housing in the area next year and we want things all nice and spick and span for them do we not?

Plate training will have to be looked at next season. As usual, the sides are determined by who is wearing what colour of shirt. Also as usual, the young 'uns all end up on one team. It means a good run around for the likes of myself but we need to mix things up and get the young 'uns used to passing to us older heads. Still, everyone seems up for Sunday and we should have twelve or thirteen players. Our opposition have tried to move this fixture because they have several players at the Paint Pot Trophy match at the Millennium Stadium. Can the mighty Rovers triumph over Doncaster in Cardiff? Can the mighty Plate take advantage of any Portcullis weakness?

Sunday 1st April 2007

Portcullis versus Avon Plate

Yate Outdoor Sports Complex Bristol & District Sunday League Division 4

Team:

Sherry

Ga Patrick Jer Pob

Bolts

Reg Korahn Yos Ned

Louis

Substitutes: (none)

Referee: Theo Wren (League appointed)

To remind me of why I am giving up the Plate Club Secretary role, this time of year is one of those periods where football and cricket begin to pull me in two directions. It was hard work getting a Plate squad together after last week's numbers turning up. I also had to attend the cricket team's trophy awards bash on the Saturday night before a game of football. Chatting to the Easton Cowboys succeeded in getting my juices flowing for the approaching cricket season. My usual opening partner was gaining Dutch courage for the speeches by slamming down spirits and salivating on our potential as a partnership. When I am chatting with the Plate, cricket goes into the background and football is all consuming. As Vice-Captain of the cricket I have to be organised at least a little for the cricket, and as Club Sec. of the Plate I am going to be very busy over the next month and a half as we see the season out and have our agm to plan. Of course, I cannot allow the situation to develop again when my mind is so distracted by sport that my family suffers unduly. This occurred at the end of last season when I was playing cricket and football, plus, trying to organize my secretarial duties, plus going away on the team-related trips to the Gower etc. It was, of course, at this stage that I take my family for granted, compartmentalize them and prioritise my need for 'me time' at their expense.

A couple of weeks ago, the Portcullis secretary had attempted to change the date of the fixture because they had players attending the Rover's match. This was supposed to be a chance for us to play a weakened team that are usually pretty good and have a very similar position to us in the league.

It was, therefore, quite distressing as one Plate player after another pulled out. Daz is in Nottingham once more. Dave is watching the Rovers. DJ James is still injured. No answer from Ali, Tyler was too done in from the night before. Lee's back is still not fixed. Jumpy is in London. The Dr is at a funeral. For the second week running, Plate have a bare eleven. Reg is carrying an ankle knock but will play. Korahn only has one boot but thankfully manages to borrow a pair, which are only a little too small for him. Thankfully, we have Patrick and Pob to come into the exact positions we need, left back and centre back. Still, we are once again unable to provide a linesman and there is no room for manoeuvre if Reg breaks down or anything untoward happens to any of the rest of us. To cap it all off, Portcullis have loads of players and most are recognisable as their first choice.

If anything can make one feel better in these circumstances, then the surroundings did just that. This sports complex is new, virgin territory for Plate. There are Astroturf pitches galore; a sophisticated looking running track (which must be thanks to the successful Olympics bid), beautiful changing rooms (although there is not enough hot water in the showers, as we were to discover) and the grass pitch we played on was top quality.

We line up for the kick off after having lost the toss; Plate will be playing the first half into the North Easterly wind. I am 'over the moon' with being picked (without any pressure or influence by me) in my favourite role as the holding midfielder. Ga has gone to right back and we are solid and brimming with talent in all other areas of the pitch. With the changes, it takes five minutes for the Plate to settle and then it is game on.

By the time twenty minutes is up, there is a feeling of déjà vu. We are creating a host of good chances, one on ones with their 'keeper and shots from within the box. None go in. Even the ref mentions to me how eerily similar to last week this was. Unfortunately, another similarity appeared. As soon as Portcullis realised we were in good form, they decided to try and bully us into submission. Without going totally over the top, their challenges pushed the laws to the limit. They were wound up further as the referee was being fair and giving us loads of free kicks. Our esteemed 'keeper is not the quickest of chaps, he just doesn't do running. With the wind at their backs, the Portcullis long balls were flying out for goal kicks and Sherry took an age in returning them. Every single Portcullis player was cussing Sherry whilst Plate were trying to explain whilst having a giggle at eleven blokes, wearing yellow, going berserk. It wasn't too long before Sherry was caught up in a car crash of a 50:50 ball. He was down for a couple of minutes, was able to continue, but only at an ever-slower pace than before. The first half had not ended when Ned also picked up a couple of knocks as he was targeted. A Portcullis bloke, standing on his foot and ankle, brought a scream from the young 'un, but that, nor a later knee-on-knee collision could stop the fella. In the midfield melee, I have their no.15 lying completely on top of me after a challenge for a header. A foot up just as I am heading the ball, hits it into my nose, no damage. Challenges where there is foot – studs – ball, bring out a shout from oneself before you have a chance to check that you haven't been broken.

Considering the conditions and the opposition, we more than hold our own with ten to one of the chances falling to Plate boots. It wasn't nearly so frustrating this week as we now know that the young 'uns get their eye in during the first half and then look far more clinical in the second. Hard work but great fun as we play our brand of the beautiful game and just keep plugging away no matter what. Half time, 0-0.

The second half and one of the main weapons used by Portcullis: long goal kicks, is nullified by the wind, now at Plate backs. Unfortunately for some of the Portcullis players, the second half is more like 'round two'; Ned is again targeted and wrestled to the ground. It is in the box, their 'keeper has it but it is a penalty to the Plate. A yellow for the defender. A red card for the sideline manager of Portcullis. Korahn ignores the delay and puts in a smartly taken penalty. 1-0 Plate.

We are playing as well as in the first half and are able to pin Portcullis back. A ball in from Ned from the left finds Yos on the edge of the box and he nonchalantly smacks it home with minimal back lift and maximum style. 2-0 Plate. The two-goal cushion is psychologically important and the celebrations are thus, wild. Short lived too. Within a minute, Sherry is tangling with the bandana-wearer of Portcullis. The tall no.9's knee clouts Sherry's thigh, Sherry's arm is tangled in his legs and down he goes. Penalty. The limping Sherry is easily beaten in the goal and there is a touch of worry about but not much as it such an isolated incident. Pob and Patrick are strong additions to the squad. Ga is having a great game at right back. Reg is soldiering on well. Ned is taking the stick and playing on. Jer is his usual solid self. Louis and Korahn are having plenty of ball and running their defence ragged and wearing them out. We also have Ali and his mate who comes to training: Nibs, as supporters. The referee won't let them on because they are not on the team sheet handed in before the game. They are very excited and vocal after watching us for a while.

The goals were coming thick and fast and Plate were quite scintillating on the attack and solid at the back. Sherry launched a goal kick, the wind carried it deep into Portcullis territory, a couple of bounces and Louis is able to sneak in, muscle their centre back off the ball and finishes with aplomb. 3-1 Plate. This is soon 4-1. Good work yet again from Korahn saw him sending in a cross that was fumbled by the Portcullis 'keeper, the ball fell to the edge of the box and Louis spun and shot and scored his first of the season with his right foot. At this point we had a good cushion and Portcullis were wilting badly. The centre began to open up and I made a couple of decent runs where the right pass would have led to goals I am sure. I had one shot narrowly wide as I charged from centre half to centre forward. Another marvellous game to be involved in.

A Portcullis breakaway saw the gap reduced to two goals. I was one of those caught well forward and could only watch as their forward rounded Sherry and hammered it in from an acute angle. I now became almost anther centre half, a la Eriksson's England when they were ahead. Portcullis had switched through various formations in the game and were now playing with most of their players in our half. They had also played some decent football in between the rough stuff and were definitely no mugs. The trio up front were able to keep the ball in the Portcullis half and eventually they were caught when their 'keeper gave away possession to the Plate and Korahn was clean through on goal. 5-2 and this was the way it stayed until the final whistle. All fight gone from Portcullis. The eleven men of Plate exhausted or injured.

'Rabbit Provencal' was the offering for the masses from The Greenbank. Plate were bunged £20 to get some takeaway stuff in and that will do nicely. We can reflect on a very fine win. Our third win in a row where the opposition have tried to kick us out of our rhythm and failed. Our third week in a row where we have given away a similar type of penalty and recovered to win. Our second win in a row with a bare eleven and without a linesman, incredibly, not even a contested decision in those two games, splendid considering we face a lot of long ball stuff against us. You would think teams would just try it on now and again, especially when desperate for a late goal, but we have been dominant in the actual possession and territory in these games and the opposition just can't get decent enough ball, with enough time, to produce killer through balls.

For a good few hours after the match, I am completely exhausted. I have a pain in my right foot. This was attained through a hard tackle or from having a perfunctory warm up and then I ran to the ref to hand in the team sheet and it gave me a bit of grief at that point. I can remember at half time thinking that there was a long way to go yet and it seemed a slog. It set me to thinking that mostly, you read that footballers, 'Wake up one morning and know it is all over'. Perhaps though, it is more insidious than that. Tiny thoughts appear in your mind that weren't there before. Little things that you wouldn't miss if you were to give it all up. The early Sunday, cold mornings. The aches and pains. The physical effort. A wee bit depressing really. Mind you, I didn't get in from the cricket do until 1.30am and was up with the lark, and the kids, a couple of hours before setting off for glory. Maybe that is why I am feeling the strain more than usual.
Man of the Match: Ga (After three rounds of voting and re-voting as he and Ned Battled it out)
Shirt of Shame: Korahn – one boot, two goals.

There are so many Plate absentees, that only ten brave souls make it to training. Three of them are not even Plate players. Jess and his chum turned up again and so we shall have to make it plain that next season is Plate only for training whatever the numbers we have. This week's session is saved as the Easton Cowboys also have ten and so we played a match against each other on the full pitch. If I were them, I would be upset as they are supposed to be preparing for a cup semi-final this weekend; at least we have the excuse of no match on Sunday.

Back Row L-R: DJ James, Patrick, Jer, Simon, Louis, Ned, Dr, Sherry, Bolts, Ali
Front Row L-R: Reg, Korahn, Jumpy, Yos, Daz, Dave

Simon, Korahn, Ned and Patrick pose for a 'Spot The ball' photo.

Half time and there is no way that Simon, myself or Patrick can be accused of taking it easy.

Style, poise and grace. Any one would do me.

The obligatory, 'Author as child with ball at feet' photo.

The above two pictures highlight the grit and determination shown by the Plate. Grrrr.

Sunday 8th April 2007

Easter Sunday and a Sunday off for the Plate. There are a couple of cup semi-finals and the odd league game going on but that's it. A good time to catch up on things.

As far as the league goes, we should be sitting nicely placed with a record of:

P	W	D	L	F	A	GD	PTS
17	9	2	6	64	49	+15	29

Unfortunately, Plate have been dealt a cruel blow. Queens Head Rangers have folded and it has been decided to expunge their results from this season's proceedings. If you are to look at the website, you cannot even see their old results, let alone see them in the table any more. It is as if they never existed. There was one team that came out of this worse than anyone else. You've guessed it, the Plate. We played them twice and beat them 7-1 and 11-0. +17 goal difference becomes –2. Thankfully, we have been on such a great run that it hasn't really knocked the stuffing out of us completely. Also, most of the other teams will lose the points and a proportion of their goal difference too.

It is a bit of a sickener. There has to be a better way of dealing with this type of situation. Oracle have leapt up the table because they were rubbish enough to lose to Queens Head, whereas we have been punished for being marvellous, seems to be the way with us. Teams like Queens must remember that their team spirit and ethos is developed in the early days. If you are just a bunch of mates, some played footy as kids, some never, some regular, then it is the days when you wonder why you bother, where you have very few numbers, when half the team seem injured, people are being sick, one is constantly aching from excursions and you are getting beaten heavily week in week out, it is here that the heart of the club is forged. If Plate are anything to go by, it takes ten seasons for a team to come of age. With the Queens, we will never know.

For the rest of us brave and organised souls, the league table for Division 4 is left looking like this:

Team	Played	Won	Drawn	Lost	For	Against	Goal difference	Points
Warwick	15	11	2	2	56	22	+34	35
Brislington 1987	14	9	3	2	56	18	+38	30
Oracle	18	8	2	8	38	27	+11	26
Longreach	14	8	1	5	44	43	+1	25
South Bristol	12	7	2	3	40	28	+12	23
Avon Plate	15	7	2	6	46	48	-2	23
Portcullis	15	6	2	7	30	42	-12	20
Cutters Friday	15	4	1	10	20	40	-20	13
Northville	15	4	1	10	19	54	-35	13
Farmhouse	13	3	3	7	19	31	-12	12
R & P Wonderboys	16	3	3	10	28	43	-15	12

We still have a lot to play for this season. Firstly, we may as well try and win all our games and pray for promotion. We also need to keep our record-breaking winning sequence going. We also need to win more games at home and thus have a fortress to protect for next season. We are building nicely for an assault on our treble for next season: GFA Minor Cup, the Charles Finch

Cup and top two promotion from whatever division we are in. There is also the top-scorer competition which is hotting up between: Louis – 14, Korahn-13, Dr –9, Yos and Ned-6 (this is only including league goals, cup goals seem to count little to the young 'uns. Perhaps this is because the FA Cup has lost so much of its lustre in recent times).

The Championship season seems to be going on forever. Derby have been unable to shake off Birmingham and Sunderland. Going into the second half of the Easter program Derby have played 41 games and are still top but are just a point ahead of Sunderland and three points above Brum who have a game in hand. The Rams are going for a record-breaking thirteenth away win in a season, still in the hunt for automatic promotion and having excellent attendances home and away. It is all so tense.

The Telegraph Fantasy League continues to hold my attention too as Avon Plate 3rd xi are still top of the work Super League and 11,335th overall. I only have three transfers left and Vidic has injured his shoulder and will be out for three – four weeks. Do I hang on to him or get another Chelsea defender in straight away? Undecided at the moment.

As for my marriage, the illnesses that have laid my wife low for a while are just beginning to clear. After years of depleting her iron and energy reserves through child-birth, breast-feeding and general child-rearing she was at an extremely low-ebb but, with regular blood tests and lots of iron in her diet, she could be over the worst. It is very hard to judge the mood and situation when someone is unwell as there is so much depression and tiredness on top of the usual amount and tends to cancel out anything good that has happened very quickly.

As far as I can tell, the decision to commit to each other has very much been made. One thing we haven't been able to do for a long time is to laugh at ourselves. We were watching the comedian: Lee Evans on the telly-box and he has been married since he and his wife were teenagers. A great deal of his act is concerned with the misunderstandings, arguments and differences between the two of them. They are very happily married but, of course, when you spend so much time together there are lots of disagreements. In his act they are extremely funny. It would be wonderful to be able to have a clear enough head to get to a place where the trials and tribulations of my family life could be seen as hilarious. However, when you are in the middle of raising a young family, one tends to be completely knackered and feeling under pressure. One doesn't want to be seen to be unable to cope at times, also, one wishes to get a rest whenever possible and so you are always trying to show that you are doing as much as your partner and deserve a sit-down. Kids screaming, fighting, messing the house up, not sleeping through the night, getting them up, putting them to bed, doing food and organising trips out and about, birthdays plus all the other celebrations to organise and pay for, being around for school holidays, getting them up and ready when school is actually running, trying to maintain some semblance of the life you had before family, illnesses, accidents, money pressures, knowing you have to hold your job down no matter what, all these things and more all act against one to make it harder to sit back, relax and keep smiling.

We are also in a frustrating period, waiting to see whether the inheritance from my Grandpa will be enough for the wife to be able to give up her job which will make her happy as she can concentrate on what she wants to do, and will lessen the physically draining effects on her and it will free up three evenings in a week thus giving me a bit more freedom and making me happier too.

My employers did manage to freeze our pay rise, cut out our 'grade-rise' too. That, with the increase in caseload, has meant that we may actually get our funding for another year. Hurrah for Mr Blair and the council cronies who seem to think that the best uses for our tax money is to spend it telling us what not to eat, what not to smoke, what not to drink, and their favourite, bloomin' little tax-collecting machines dotted all over our roads: speed cameras. It is a little galling when police spending goes up even though they couldn't detect if their own noses are running let alone solving a crime. Let's cut my lots' funding even though it seems to achieve actual results. It is quite annoying to think that I must pay more this year via council tax to the very same people who have decided to reduce my wages.

This week has seen me again struggling with the juggling of my roles as Plate Club Secretary and the vice-captaincy for the coming cricket season. This past week, Jumpy has called to inform me that we no longer have Monks Park booked for training so what to do? A frantic couple of days of communicating with the team and we have switched it to Eastville Park, it is free, it is grass, there is enough daylight.

When I rang Frys Club to check on this weekend's match, there are no pitches available. A stressful time follows and we end up with a pitch but no changing rooms. Northville are contacted and they are ok with the situation. Again, masses of communications are sent out so that we are aware and ready for the situation. Let us just hope it doesn't rain on Sunday. Next, an email is received from Patrick to say that he has pulled a groin muscle and will be out for a couple of weeks at least. More communications follow as I try and ensure we have enough players. We also have to find a goalkeeper as Sherry's ban has kicked in and the referee that sent him off will be somewhere at Frys. There are also several of the team that do not want to play him anyway as he should serve out his punishment and learn his lesson. Finally, the Greenbank pub has shut for improvements, unfortunately, where the landlord had said two weeks, what he meant was two months. This means rearranging the Plate AGM. This will require meetings with landlords and more organising. Thus, where I could really do with a situation where the footy is running smoothly and I can handle the dual demands of cricket and footy, the Plate remain hard work and time-consuming, bless them.

It has reminded me of the need to resign from Club Secretary duties at the AGM. As at end of training night on Thursday, we have the Plough pub in Easton as a probable AGM venue and they are happy to have us on Sundays whilst the Greenbank is shut, training went very well as The Cowboys have joined us and we can have a proper friendly every mid week to the end of the season, thirteen players have confirmed for Sunday, still no 'keeper though.

Sunday 15th April 2007

Avon Plate versus Northville Athletic

Frys Club, Keynesham
Bristol & District Sunday League Division 4

Team:

		Sherry		
Ga	Reg		Jer	Pob
		Bolts		
Tyler	Dr		Korahn	Ned
		Louis		

Substitutes: Ali (for me 70 mins)
Dave (for Ga 75 mins)
Daz (for Pob 80 mins)

Referee: M Popel (League appointed)

The usual frustration for myself before a game: arrive at Ned's, wait around for him to get ready. Next, on to Tyler and Korahn's to wait around for even longer whilst they decide whether they are too buggered from the night before, is there going to be enough kit for them to beg and borrow, finally we can set off for Frys'. Good news upon arrival at the ground though, we do have a changing room and the pitch is lovely if a bit slopey. Jer and myself have a word with the ref about Sherry. We haven't heard anything from his leniency plea for his ban and the ref thus says he can play. Therefore, even without Patrick, Lee, Jumpy and James B (all injured) nor Yos (ill), we have a decent looking squad with the balance to cover most eventualities. It is nice to have a full turn out again and we shall even have the luxury of a linesman.

This is a rematch of the 26th November 2006 game, one I had been dreading as it felt more like 'Round 2' than simply the second league meeting of the season. However, recent weeks' events have meant that it is a perfect time to test our new resolve, strength and guts. Personally I am pleased to be handed the holding midfielder role and I had a say in the team selection concerning right back. More honour was heaped onto my slender shoulders with captaincy of the Plate for a day. I use my team talk to warn the Plate of the inevitability of Northville using physical tactics as soon as they see we are going to try and play proper football. Plate win the toss and I decide to kick down the slope for the first half. My thinking is that Jer has called for more first half goals, so go with the slope. Also, we will be fit and raring to go with the slope and by the time Northville get to use it, they will be, hopefully, half beaten and knackered anyway and Plate are usually very good in the second half thus negating the slope advantage.

We start well. The captaincy drives me to set an early example and two shots of mine go close in the first few minutes. Another couple of half chances go begging and we wonder if this is going to be another typical Plate script. However, Tyler picks up a cross field ball, use his pace to get away from his marker, cuts inside another Northville defender and taps it in past the now stranded 'keeper. 1-0 to the Plate and we are well on top.

Although we have gone 'off-script' by scoring early in the first half, we learn our lines in time to give another penalty away. Our fourth pen against, in four weeks. This time the culprit is my good self. Northville take a corner that leads to a bit of a scramble, their guy wins it and shoots. I try and use my chest to turn the ball round the corner but I am falling over and end up with my arm landing on the ball. They score the penalty to make it 1-1.

The game begins to settle into a pattern: Plate with most of the good possession and passing with Northville grunting and groaning around us and launching the odd ball forward in a fairly dangerous manner. Our young 'uns are combining well and on twenty minutes Louis sets Korahn away, a shot across the 'keeper and we are back in front 2-1. I notice that once the ball gets to one of the young 'uns, they are tending to speed off and create merry hell. Unfortunately, they are going forward with such pace that both Dr and myself are being left behind and so are ending up both playing the holding role. With Jer's permission, I move out to right midfield and Tyler pushed into the centre as a more advance midfielder playing in the Rooney-type role behind Louis.

From this point on, Plate are amazing. I have never witnessed us passing the ball across the back, stringing together ten passes in a move, movement off the ball and looking like we are a team that knows what it is doing. A couple of minutes after our second goal, and the Plate play comes to a glorious fruition. I tackle a Northville chap and knock it to Ned, first time ball to Korahn, first time ball to myself, first time ball onto Louis who squares it beautifully, my left foot cocks back but Tyler nips in to smash the ball home. A beautiful feeling flows through me, and seemingly the rest of the Plate, literally a goal that Man Utd would have been proud to score.

Again though, we take our 'eyes off the prize' and, on the stroke of half time, a straight forward move of Northville's sees our defenders trying to fall over near to their players but this does not put them off and they score to make it 3-2 to Plate at half time.

There is a slight worry going into the second half, we haven't managed to kill off Northville and we now have to play up the slope. The first ten minutes of the half turn out to be Plate heaven. Three goals from us, in the space of a few minutes, all of them crackers. A Ned throw-in goes to Dr who passes to a centrally placed Korahn, he moves it into Louis' feet who touches the ball round his marker and smacks it into the bottom corner. 4-2. Ned, Dr, and Louis combine to play Korahn down the line, he squares it to Tyler, is he going to pass to me in space in front of goal? No, he will score his hat trick goal instead. 5-2. Tyler and Korahn play a one-two, which sees Korahn through; will he pass it to me in space in front of Goal? No, he finishes with aplomb instead. 6-2 to the Plate.

At this point, the mood of the match changes for the worse. At the beginning of the half, Northville were hopeful. When we began to rip them to shreds, their heads went down, they lost their shape and were giving up. At 6-2, their goalie decides to show his feelings by lying down in their box, Reg pipes up with,'Who beached the whale?' and the mood turned from one of Northville resignation to Northville rage. For a few tension-filled minutes the referee is able to maintain control. Unfortunately, Reg then mis-times a challenge and goes right through on one of their blokes. After a couple of minutes of verbals, the Northville 'keeper drags himself up the pitch and attempts to land one on Reg. In trying to get to Reg, the 'keeper has to flail about at Sherry and then Jer. Meanwhile, another of their players grabs hold of Pob, he is having none of that and so puts the Northville lad into a headlock instead. Pob's father had come to see him for the first time in Plate colours and I am sure was mightily impressed with what he was seeing. Luckily, the last few weeks have shown that if we just carry on with our game then we win and so we try and calm the situation. I am quite glad that nobody gets sent off or that would have prolonged the trouble and there would have been a very good chance of another abandonment, knowing our luck we would have somehow lost the points and all. Once the adrenalin, red mist and frustration have drained out of the Northville lads, we can get back on with the match. With everything calmed down, the match spends its last fifteen minutes ambling to a finish.

I am substituted on seventy-five minutes for Ali who looks pretty good. I am able to witness several more Plate moves that consist of phases-of-play from front-to-back, lots of movement and first time passing, lovely. Dave comes on for Ga five minutes later, he squares straight up to a Northville lad after their first tackle, but he is no trouble and keeps his mouth in check. Daz comes on for Pob. Daz makes it seem like he has entered a military zone of late '60's Vietnam. Every tackle sees him in a groaning heap calling for the medic. Although there are some lame efforts, Northville do not manage to extract any further retribution from Reg. In the final moments, they score another scrappy goal from a corner. The final score is 6-3 to the Plate.

The Greenbank is shut and we don't have a clue as to when it will reopen its doors and so it is off to the Plough for the rest of the season. There is no real hardship except that we lose any food we might have got from the Greenbank, otherwise though, the beer is very cheap, there are lots of telly-boxes showing cricket and football and there is a 'garden' where we can pursue our recreational activities without bother. Any pub would be okay today though after another fine win. Four wins a row for the first time ever. Four matches that we have won whilst the opposition attempt to kick us out of our stride, four games with penalties given against us, four times we have taken the physical conditions and turned them to our advantage.
Man of the Match: Tyler – 'Hat-trick hero' (a special mention must go for my one vote for the, 'dream goal involvement'.
Shirt of Shame: Reg - 'Starting a war', 'Dancing around the fat bloke', 'Fanning the flames of destruction'.

A monumental training session for Ned as we witness the birth of a nickname. On Sunday, in the heat and sweat, his hair went all curly and some of the Northville lads started to call him, ‘Poodle’. After another hot and sweaty session of training, we had the reappearance of the poodle style. At some point, Ned exclaimed that he was, ‘Not a poodle’, this was soon a spoonerism for, ‘Pot Noodle’, and this shall be his footy name from now on.

Almost as monumental is that more players want to join us but we have a pretty large and strong squad already. Do we close the squad list? We did expect that, as the original Platers are retired, the new players will be based more on skill and talent than on the friendships that led to the creation of the Plate in the first place, but players like myself don’t want to be sidelined quite so soon.

Sunday 22nd April 2007

Cutters Friday Reserves versus Avon Plate

Cutters Club, Stockwood
Bristol & District Sunday league Division 4

Team:

Sherry
Bolts Patrick Jer Pob
Dr
Tyler Korahn Yos Ned
Louis

Substitutes: Reg (for Yos 75mins)
Ga (unused sub – linesman)
Ali (unused sub)
Dave (unused sub)

Referee: no league appointed referee.

Playing in the afternoon certainly feels quite surreal. It gives one too much time, you end up checking your kitbag several times and looking at the clock too much. I had a weekend of being very 'grown up' and cleared the garden shed (one single bed base, a double-bed frame, a wooden cot, several glass jars, some dried out paint pots, a few oil containers, damp blankets, garden tools, thousands of cobwebs and dead woodlice amongst other things to chuck away), this meant I didn't think about the match until suddenly it was time to go and pick up the young 'uns. Even then it didn't feel like a footy day until all the Plate had arrived.

Cutters are in the envious position of having their own pitch and clubhouse with a bar. Although there has been no rain for weeks, the pitch took a stud, as the ground was so crumbly that your boots could still dig into the ground with ease. Plate have fifteen players on show plus a crowd consisting of Dan, Jumpy plus a fair number of Jer's family members. Cutters have a similar amount on the sidelines. No league referee but this can be a blessing. Again I am back to right back but there is no longer too much disappointment at that, the way the team is shaping up I will not have many choices in future I would imagine. It was imperative for me to warm up more than usual as I was feeling stiff as a board. There was also pain in my right foot as my athlete's foot has been raging lately. Luckily, the blisters began weeping as I got ready and the pain lessened (nice). So, all in all, a good chance today, to gain revenge for a defeat against Cutters earlier in the season and keep the record, winning run going.

Today, as in the previous game, Cutters have at least half a team of their Saturday / first team players on show. Thankfully, I don't have any hang-ups any more with regards reserve teams. Part of the growing up process that we have witnessed with this season's Plate is not to worry about the personnel we are facing. If we are ambitious then we must be good enough, and not keep blaming factors other than ourselves.

Yos is back to being captain but there is no pressure on the toss as the pitch is flat and there is very little wind. Plate are straight into their stride. It is nice for us to show Yos a little of what he missed last week in terms of possession and attacking flair. Within five minutes we have had a couple of clear chances, not put them away but not too frustrated yet.

Cutters are good. Their top players want to get the ball down and play, it is only the minority of their guys who slice and hoof the ball. Their first-teamers are also pretty tough, unfortunately, these players want to play up front and so their defence was weak, hence our increasing number of spurned chances. It is a fair old struggle at right back, they are quick to double-up on me when they are in possession, Tyler is playing as advanced as possible and struggles to get goal-side. It is a similar position on the Plate left flank too. As the game becomes even, I want to assert myself and leap into a difficult header against their winger. I don't know how, but I am caught in the face by something very hard. It could have been an elbow, or boot, or forehead. Whatever the offending item, it was excruciatingly painful. Unlike the Premiership stars, I didn't go down sobbing, instead I kept wiping the blood away and pulling the flapping skin away from the inside of my mouth. Soon enough there was another 50:50 challenge with the same players involved and there was no way I was going to be bullied out of the match. Ball won, Cutter on the floor, no blood but I'm back in control on the right.

Plate chances come and go with depressing regularity, Cutters play a long ball that bounces on the edge of our box, Pob begins to shield it from their attacker but where is Sherry? Eventually, Pob plays the ball back but this is just after Sherry has decided to move off his line after all. Pob's pass manages to sneak by Sherry and the Cutters attacker accepts the gift. A good deal of the Plate attacks are failing because we are trying to be Arsenal and pass it into the net, Cutters show that, until a couple of goals ahead, scoring the 'dirty' goals can set you going just as well as the 'flashy' ones.

It is with devastating play that Plate surge up field, see a lovely interchange between the young 'uns, and watch the net bulge from yet another Korahn finish. 1-1.The rest of the half consists of Plate in charge although not ripping them apart. Thus, our half time team talk concentrates on Cutters giving it a good go for ten minutes as they will be surprised and delighted to be level.

From the Plate restart, we pass it through their team and miss another glorious chance; great start to the half though. Not really, with their first attack of the half, Cutters win a corner, which is poorly defended. A Cutters attacker has the time in our box to turn and shoot the ball into the net, just above my head as I stand on the post. 1-2 but forty minutes to go.

Although the day is hot, and the pitch is large, my energy levels are increasing throughout the game. It cannot all be down to the can of half time Red Bull. Instead of adrenalin pumping through my veins and spurring me on, large doses of frustration fuel me instead. Plate continue to create excellent possession in the Cutters' box, there are too many passes being attempted by the Plate attack and our windows of opportunity close. There are untold one on one situations, with Louis the most guilty party it must be said, all were wasted. Personally, there was a cross that was nipped off Yos' head, a cross that looped and bounced on the six-yard line but went out for a goal kick. This highlights that Plate are now a resilient team, a skilful team, but not one that does the 'dirty' stuff well: The putting the foot through the ball on clearances, not letting the ball bounce, not taking responsibility for the finish or to hold possession and in this case, the desire to knock in a goal with any part of the body because, as a striker, you want to gamble and throw yourself into an area that is dangerous. It is not all about the glory strikes.

As we entered the last ten minutes, the call went up to, 'Raise our game Plate'. This did not really seem possible as we were already creating chances every couple of minutes. The Cutters forward line had been starved of possession. Reg came on for Yos and it was clear that fresh legs were a good thing. I for one found it hard to keep supporting his runs into the channel and the chances kept on coming and going. At one point I was joking with the Plate crowd (thank goodness they were there to keep us smiling and trying) with an imaginary girlfriend of the young 'uns saying, 'Finish me, baby, finish me.' and the young 'uns having to reply that they, 'did not know how to finish'. We laughed anyway. I did try to speak to Jer at one point about the substitutes but I was so out of puff and the game was going on that I didn't have the chance to say anything useful. The one real negative to come out of the match was that Ga, Dave and Ali were all unused subs.

The referee, who there has been no need to mention as he was such a commanding presence and quick and firm with his decisions, blew for full time. Football, being a funny old game, has let the 'best team lose' (Cutters' words not mine particularly).

As Cutters have such fine facilities, and the Greenbank is still closed for refurbishment, we decide to have a drink with the gracious victors. Respect is due to Louis who faced up to what had happened. We chatted and hopefully it is a positive development. At least he has played in a game and missed chances in a match that is not going to decide promotion. Everything we are doing is to get us ready for an assault next season, so to get a game like this out of his system now, with his brain never wanting to go through the experience again, will stand him in good stead for the future.

Shirt of Shame: Sherry – 'First goal blunder' (Pot Noodle and Louis got a couple of votes for glaring misses, Jer some, for not using substitutes and Reg some, for voting slowly).

Man of the Match: Pob – After a revote with Patrick, both for their solid defending and attitude.

The last feelings of frustration were soon gone once we had arrived at the Plough as we joined the celebrating Easton Cowboys Sunday team, the Charles Finch Cup winners 2007, in a cuddle, a sing, and some jovial banter.

Sunday 29th April 2007

Brislington 1987 versus Avon Plate

Imperial Ground
Bristol & District Sunday League Division 4

Team:

Sherry
Ga Patrick Jer Ned
Bolts
Yos Korahn Dr Louis
Tyler

Substitutes: Ali (for Ga 75 mins)

Referee: G. Miles (league appointed)

After working hard for the past couple of weeks to prepare for today's two games, we end up with just twelve for this morning with Pob and Dan coming along for the afternoon fixture with South Bristol Wanderers. Reg disappeared off the face of the planet, Dave is working, Daz is in Nottingham, Jumpy and James B are unfit and getting over knocks and Lee is out for a while still with his bad back. Thankfully, Sherry is okay to play as his ban has been put off until next season and, today, we have the same referee that sent him off. As numbers seem to be dwindling, perhaps it is good that the season is coming to an end.

Today is a great chance to see how far we have come this season and give a clue as to what may be in store for us next season in terms of promotion chances. Brislington are top and are promoted, thus, if we can match them we will be in great shape.

With our three left backs all out, Ned is shifted to the position, Yos has a new position and I am back to holding midfield (I think that this is in response to my going to play cricket in the afternoon, he is giving me a running around role to use my energy for the morning, good for the Plate but not so for my ageing body). Louis and Tyler are in different positions too as a response to our lack of finishing the last few weeks.

We kick off on a properly hot day. With the tiny bit of rain we have had recently, it has stopped the ground crumbling so the pitch is properly hard. There is certain slickness on show but that is the football this fine morning. The good news is that a lot of this play is coming from the Plate. For the first forty minutes, the titanic battle remains at 0-0. The referee hardly has to do anything, just two great teams slugging it out. Yet again, Plate create the lion's share of chances but it is never one-way traffic. In the pre-match team talk, Jer had spoken of shooting earlier and in this game, perhaps the young 'uns have taken this directive too far but as part of our learning curve, this is no bad thing. What does begin to cost us is that we are playing too directly. We are able to pass it out from the back but once it enters midfield we are playing it along the line or looking for the killer ball. Obviously, this has much to do with the way Brislington are closing us down, but the result is disjointed play for the Plate.

After my recent bouts of frustrated shouting (which had annoyingly crept into this week's training session too) I was determined just to enjoy the game and be positive. However, this was tested to the limit as half time approached. Much of the Brislington joy was being caused via their speedy winger up against Ga. Playing far too tight, the Brislington guy is able to spin off Ga and accelerate away from him. The pitch is quite small and so when this occurs, their chap is in a good position to take the ball on a few yards and shoot. With five minutes remaining of the half, it is too late to coach Ga, their bloke does his trick again and this time shoots and scores. 0-1, half time.

The half time team talk is again quite difficult. Our play is good and we are creating chances, plus we are restricting Brislington. Not much can be said except for us to play more square balls and build a little slower which will give our midfield a chance to support our attacks.

For a good half hour, the match is locked at 0-1, Plate are playing even better this half. The Brislington 'keeper is having a great game (why does this keep happening against us?) and the tension is growing in the opposition ranks. Finally, inevitably, there is a goal. A long ball from Brislington is shepherded by Jer back into our box, Jer calls for Sherry to come and get it, 'No thanks', is the reply and thus Jer decides to leave the ball anyway. The only person who wants to take responsibility is the Brislington forward who steals in between our two shirkers and bashes it in. 0-2 and it makes you want to cry.

Once the arguments between manager and 'keeper have died down it is back to the match. We press, torment, tackle, pass, cross and shoot in wave upon wave of Plate great play. Ga makes way for Ali with the final quarter approaching. Dr is now switched up front with Yos going into centre-mid and Ali out on the right. I am back to right back so at least their threat over there is now over. The Dr becomes the most threatening player on the pitch and with five minutes to go he scores a peach of a goal with a thirty-yard shot. 1-2.

It is now frantic stuff. The Brislington defence is good enough to repel any long ball attacks and we miss some disgracefully easy chances. Ali is his usual gazelle-like self but he has no footballing head on today. He receives the ball in acres of space and time but slashes wildly at everything. The poor guy obviously needs a pre-season with us and to get some more time on the pitch.

When the final whistle blows on a 2-1 victory for Brislington, there is handshaking galore. Unlike so many of our recent games, there has been no violence and no cards, just a plethora of football skills that would have done justice to a much higher level of football. Again, I would say 'The best team lost'. As a team we have learnt a bit more about each other's play. The young 'uns are a bit more experienced and us older 'uns are working out how best to link with the voices of the new generation. We have certainly proven that we are already at a level where we can push for promotion next season. Lovely.

More good news for myself especially, and the Plate as a whole. The South Bristol secretary gives me a bell to inform us that they don't have a fit team to put out and will forfeit the match and hand us the points. I am in no doubt that we would have taken them to the cleaners with eleven on eleven let alone eleven on eight. I can now head off to cricket with no guilt or wishing I was with the Plate for the afternoon.

Shirt of Shame: Ali – 'Comedy Shorts'

Man of the Match: Dr – 'Sets high standards and met them'

Derby County seem to be in the same boat as Plate. We have built for next season and Derby are doing the same. No automatic promotion as we lost at Palace to send Birmingham (boo) and Sunderland (not boo) into the Premiership. The consolation is that if Derby does well, I can have a legitimate reason to visit the new Wembley and if we don't get promoted then next season could be another winning and exciting one for the Rams. Next weekend sees Derby play out the season against the doomed Leeds United and their thuggish bunch of 'fans'. Oh, how proud they must be to have been relegated with their, 'good name' dragged through the Portman Road mud. The supposed majority of Leeds fans who actually follow their team's fortunes on the pitch rather than looking for the elderly and children's faces to be rearranged, were quite rightly apologetic about their 'supporters' behaviour but the longer they stay out of the limelight the better, just a reminder but it is 2007 and not 1977.

As the Rams were letting me down, the Cowboys were making me proud. Utterly fatigued in the brain and body, I was only able to contribute seven runs as opener. Unfortunately, two other wickets had already gone down before mine (this caused my brain to overheat and lose focus). We recovered slightly, went back into trouble, recovered slightly again and were all out for a seemingly hopeless 136. Excellent captaincy from Dean, with myself cajoling, comforting and shouting in my Vice-Captain role, we managed to skittle Peasedown out for 133, very exciting. By the time I got back from celebrating at the Plough I must admit to feeling terribly, terribly tired.

Sunday 6th May 2007

Oracle versus Avon Plate

Eastville Park Bristol & District Sunday League Division 4

Team:

Sherry

Bolts Patrick Jer Ga

Dr Yos Korahn

Tyler Louis Ned

Substitutes: Ali (For Tyler 60 mins)
Pob (For Ga 65 mins)
Nibs/ Niv (For Dr 80 mins)

Referee: T Wren (League appointed)

The final game of the season. Jer decides to play another new formation and shift the personnel around one last time as there is no promotion / relegation issues to be settled. Also, this formation could stop the Oracle defence from hoofing the ball as much as usual. However, Plate do have things to play for today: (1) If we win or draw we will finish above Oracle. (2) We continue to build for next season's assault. (3) We will finish fourth in the league (perhaps even a true third as Longreach will finish above us but we had the abandonment a few weeks ago) (4) If we win we will finish with a positive goal difference. (5) If we win, we can go into the AGM with pride and satisfaction.

(6) Perhaps most importantly, there is a guy called Tom in their defence who works for the same bunch of pay-cutters that I do and thus there is a lot of pride at stake for us.

After much, last-minute, ringing around, we manage to sort out a full squad of fourteen players and a small crowd of Plate well-wishers. Oracle can only muster the bare eleven. At least we have a proper referee to end the season on and it is nice to have the incomprehensible but rather good, Theo.

Thankfully, the weather is not as hot as last week and I can thus look forward to playing an attacking and pushing-on full back role without knackering myself too much for the cricket later. The ground is well hard though and I haven't brought any other footwear than my normal boots. Still, I have more stuff than the young 'uns, who even now are still scratching around for boots, socks and shorts. Almost as if they want to win the shirt of shame.

To be honest, Plate do not click straight from the off. There are good signs all over the pitch. Korahn is playing well with Yos and Dr looking after the midfield shape around him. Louis is making lots of runs in the space out left with Ned buzzing around and picking up the pieces. Myself and Ga are able to push on as we hoped. Jer and Patrick are solid and assured as ever. Tyler is causing damage but lacking his usual cutting edge. The first half hour is not even by any means but Oracle are competitive in this match. Their secretary is a lovely bloke who also possesses a lot of speed and is the only one who can maintain the energy levels required to hold us. Gradually, his influence is diminished as Yos decides to give him no mercy in the tackle and the rest of us continue to wear down the Oracle resistance. Perhaps a turning point comes when the Oracle number 10 (who I had been tussling with) has to go into goal with an injury and the 'keeper moves up front. At this point I am able to really start playing as an extra midfielder as I had things under control before and now am well on top in my area of the pitch.

Things begin to turn a bit déjà vu again as Oracle hold onto the 0-0. Finally, the ball is worked through the middle and Tyler plays a lovely ball into our right-hand channel, I charge onto it and decide to cross to the far post. It hangs, it arrows toward the top corner and in! This time Korahn decides not to try and finish it off and so it counts. A goal for our hero. 'That's the way to do it', I gleefully inform our forwards. Even better, the Easton Cowboys Sunday team is playing on the next pitch to us and so some of the cricket team and other well-known faces are about and they have seen my goal, what a rush.

Half time, 1-0 to Plate. I have to remove my undergarment from beneath my shirt as it is dripping wet with sweat. It is not looking good for my energy levels later. A can of Red Bull and I am ready for the second half. I definitely do not want to get substituted today as I am enjoying myself so much and this is it for months. First, we have to get the Dr's moaning out of the way. For some reason he is not taking advice well today and the centre midfield is the final piece of the jigsaw that needs to get sorted.

The second half and it is 'next goal wins' time. If we can get two goals up then surely there will be no way back for Oracle. We don't have long to wait. A Plate corner swings in from the left, Korahn has an easy header but it hits the defender, loops up and Korahn heads it again and this time the ball sneaks across the line before another defender makes sure it is definitely a goal for the Plate.

It becomes clear now that only their secretary has not given up. From the restart, he dribbles through us and has a shot which brings out the only save needed from Sherry all game. Soon enough, we are awarded a free kick out on the right. Lou, Yos and Ned stand over it before Yos peels infield to the edge of the D. The resulting cross was half cleared and it fell to Yos on the half volley. His sweet right-foot shot arrows into the top corner as straight as a dye, it was close to the 'keeper but it was past him before he could move. Yos' 'jazz hands' celebration is not enough to get him the Shirt of Shame but is priceless nonetheless. 3-0 to Plate.

As we continue to pile on the pressure, I have a sneaky watch of how old Tom is getting on for Oracle. He is playing opposite me as their right back but he is having a torrid time with Ned and Louis. His face is red and his cheeks are puffed out. Oracle cannot get any sort of pressure or possession of their own and Plate take advantage. Another free kick on the right is taken by Ned who swings it in high. The ball clears everyone except for the predatory Yos who finishes well from all of two yards. 4-0 becomes 5-0. Pob (who has come on for Ga in part of a double substitution) takes a throw-in into the Oracle box, Korahn fights off the challenges and takes the ball to the by-line, cuts inside, twists his ankle, and passes to Louis who slots it into the bottom left corner of their net. Korahn is obviously in pain but we have just made two substitutes and Nibs (new player, friend of Ali's) is not ready to come on. Also, Louis scoring has now put himself and Korahn level for the 'Golden Boot' award. Korahn's decision as to whether he can continue is decided when Louis makes it 6-0 to the Plate and for a time becomes our highest scorer this season.

With ten minutes to go, the Golden Boot is decided. Intense Plate pressure gives me another opportunity to get forward and my shot is cleared for a Plate corner. I take it because I am near the ball and everyone is running out of juice. My corner is cleared off Dr's head for another Plate set piece. There is no way I am going to run right across the pitch to take this corner and so leave it to Louis who simply places the ball onto an unmarked Korahn's head for an easy goal. 7-0 to the Plate. There is time for one more golden opportunity but crazily, Korahn gives up the chance of a hat trick to set Ned up who promptly misses and the game is over.

There is much backslapping from the two old foes and we promise to continue our seasons-long battle into the next campaign. A handshake for the shattered (physically and mentally) Tom. A quick doobie and I have to leave the celebrations, for cricket over in Cadbury Heath. I wish I could have partied with the Plate as I end up absolutely knackered fielding for the Cowboys and then making a nought at bat. The weather may have been nice and chilly for footy but it was not pleasant for the cricket.

Shirt of Shame: Louis – No shorts

Man of the Match: Yos – two goals and 'worked hard'

Post – Season Analysis:

What I thought would be my last season as a player endeth. The Gods of football have inspired me though; I hope to go on for another two or three seasons yet. It would be marvellous to be playing with the young 'uns as they mature and gain experience to go with their undoubted talent and energy. There are enough of us now that it takes the pressure off my old bones. No more playing in the depths of winter with ten men let's hope. We lost: Craig, Lewis, Tony, Simon, Drew, Joff, Ross and Dan from our season-start playing personnel. We recruited: The young 'uns of Ned, Louis, korahn and Tyler plus Ali, Patrick and Pob. Apart from lacking a reserve goalkeeper, Plate's squad appears to be in great shape for the future. We will have to decide whether to put a limit to newcomers rather than fearing for the end of the Plate.

The Bristol & District Sunday League Division 4 ended thusly:

11 Team	Games Played	Games Won	Games Drawn	Games Lost	Games For	Goals Against	Goals Difference	Points
Brislington 1987	20	14	4	2	77	23	+54	**49**
Warwick	20	15	2	3	83	25	+58	**47**
Longreach Athletic Reserves	20	12	1	7	53	58	-5	**37**
Avon Plate	20	10	2	8	61	55	+6	**42**
Oracle	20	8	2	10	41	43	-2	**26**
Portcullis	20	8	2	10	40	56	-16	**26**
Cutters Friday Reserves	20	8	2	10	31	45	-14	**23**
South Bristol Wanderers	20	7	2	11	43	70	-27	**23**
Farmhouse	20	5	5	10	37	41	-4	**20**
Northville Athletic Reserves	20	6	2	12	30	65	-35	**20**
R&P Oldboys	20	3	4	13	30	45	-15	**13**

We can feel some pride at having a 'winning' season (more games won than lost) with the only positive goal difference outside of the top two. We finished above Oracle. Plate scored a tremendous amount of quality goals.

What I will take most from this season though, is the way we have grown up as a team that is now capable of really competing on a Sunday morning. So many incidents have happened in games this season. Early on, these things, such as weather conditions, the performance of the referee, not having a ref, intimidation, abandonments, all had a negative affect on us. We would lose the game against an inferior side and have plenty of good reasons to bemoan our luck in the pub afterwards. Once we had clicked and gelled, Plate began to turn these adversities into wins. We have a solid and brave spine to the team. There is also a lot more knowledge with regards the game, craft and art of the game of football within our squad now. Punches have been thrown, more inclement weather, referees perhaps having an off day, no referees, good referees, more intimidation, but we keep on going now until the job is done and in a spirit that has most of us shaking hands at the end of a match.

Financially, the Plate are in reasonable shape. We have some money for the AGM to be a really good time and the trophies are of a higher quality than last year's. Hopefully our sponsorship with The Greenbank and Bristol Beer Factory will continue and we don't have to fork out for a new kit this year.

I completed my final (I hope) duty as Club Secretary of the Plate on 9th June 2007 by chairing the AGM. With three bottles of Tequila and the majority of the Plate on show it was destined to be a fun day out in the Plough's garden. As this is the 7th Plate AGM that I have been involved in and organised, it only took three hours and we were through the business part of the day and onto the all-important awards:

Most Appearances: Sherry – Played in every minute of our 23 games this season, even waiting until the whistle had gone versus Oracle before getting sent off (see below).
Most Shirt of Shame awards: Sherry – See above.
'Wrong Ray' – (For 'comedy moment'): **Ned** – For breaking the trophy during the meeting.
Golden Boot': Louis & Korahn - 18 goals each.

Best Goal: Tyler – For the best goal I have ever had the pleasure to be involved in versus Northville.
Clubman: Bolts – My usual award I'm afraid but it does show that the Plate still recognise my work and obviously love me very much. I would like to think that I might figure for some of the other awards next year, as I won't be a shoe-in for this trophy any more.
Best Newcomer: Patrick – Never a doubt as to who was going to win this one
Most Improved Player: Ned – As he trained a couple of times with us last season he won this award rather than be up for best newcomer.
Players' Player: Korahn – Even though he thought the meeting was tomorrow and was therefore unable to accept his award in person, he fully deserves his accolade.

Ready for the AGM, but is Yos ready to assume his position of new Club Secretary?

Sherry joins in for some abuse of power at the 'Top Table'

Jer tries to buy votes for another year of management (successfully).

I managed twenty games in which I was subbed twice, I also managed four goals, well I say four goals, I think that this is putting it mildly when you consider the scorcher of a left foot into the top corner versus Farmhouse, how about the equaliser from the half way line versus Warwick, or the cheeky chip from the edge of the box versus Oracle). The final stats for the team were as follows:

Name	Full Games	As sub (subbed)	Goals (cup)
Bolts	21	(2)	4
Yos	15	(3)	8
Sherry	23	-	-
Reg	16	-	-
Dr	19	-	10 (5)
Dave	8	3	-
Lee	6	1 (1)	1
Daz	7	2 (3)	-
Simon	6	2	-
DJ James	1	8 (2)	1 (1)
Ned	15	4 (2)	6 (1)
Korahn	14	-	18
Louis	15	(4)	17 (1)
Tyler	4	2 (1)	4
Dan	1	-	-
Ali	3	8	1
Jer	20	1	(1)
Jumpy	8	2 (3)	2
Ga	3	2 (10)	1
Tony	1	1	-
Craig	2	(1)	-
Patrick	7	-	2
Pob	2	3 (1)	-

The Plate story may be very exciting and full of wonder, but we would be hard pushed to give our fans the sort of excitement that Derby County are this season. After the marathon 46 games of the Championship season, we lost out to Birmingham by two measly points and have to go through the play-offs. Of course, as we finished clearly third, us Rams will argue that the play-offs are rubbish and that we deserve to go up. Unfortunately, the play-offs are here to stay so we must live with heart-rending matches. It was intense to say the least as Ga and Yos plus Sherry and myself watched the deciding leg of the semi-final against Southampton. Apart from myself in Derby top and Ga who was obviously Derby, the rest of the crowd in the Plough pub took great pleasure in supporting the Saints. Throughout the match, as Derby continuously seemed to sew the tie up, only for saints to come back, it was bloomin' annoying listening to the jeers and screams but when Derby scored themselves it was an adrenalin fuelled ride all right. By the time the match had finished 4-4 on aggregate and extra time had been played out, I was jumping up and down like a loon on the pub's furniture but as I was outnumbered so much, and it was the landlord's birthday, I could get away with a bit of lairy behaviour. Thank goodness Ga was there as back up though or it would have been unbearable. Penalties are an awful way to finish a match, even though that is how we finally disposed of the Southampton menace. Most of the people I know would argue that taking a player off every few minutes in extra time would be a better way of doing it but for the foreseeable future it will not change. It was heart-warming to witness Seth Johnson back as a starting midfielder in such an important match. It looks like he has convinced Billy Davies of his worth. Seth is our Robbie Fowler, a fairytale that is so rare in football. Sherry was also touched because he is a Crewe fan and another Seth-lover. After the match I had to stop over at Yos' before driving home as I was so wired and by the time I reached home and had relived it all with the missus I came crashing down from an extended adrenalin high. What a night.

The feelings were only exacerbated when Yeovil trashed Forest and so our rivals will not be going to the new Wembley before us after all, shame. Poor old Daz.

The FA Cup final at the new Wembley was a real letdown. As a father and husband, I make the effort to try and get the family into football, they sit and watch, and the only words are: 'frustrating', 'boring' and 'annoying'. Both teams had already won silverware this season (Man Utd the Premiership and Chelsea the League Cup), it was the first proper match for the new stadium and thus, we should have had a game, surely, where both managers would instruct their teams to 'have a go' and really put down markers for next season. However, Mourinho chose to 'Enjoy after the match', and not the match itself. Fine, but what about the millions of us watching and the potential long-term damage to the game if these pitiful matches were to continue in the high profile, and most watched, games. For the record, Chelsea snatched a 1-0 victory in extra time.

The Champions League had the potential to be a dull affair, with the 'tactical genius' of Rafa Benitez and his defensive tactics on show. However, the game was reasonable although no classic by any means. Liverpool were on top until Inzaghi scored just before half time. His second killed Liverpool's chances although there were five minutes of nerves as Liverpool scored to make it 1-2 and threaten a turnaround as in 2005, but not this time. Gerrard was speaking in a Plate-like fashion by stating that he wasn't too disappointed as Liverpool were definitely, 'on the up'.

In fantasyland, it all got a bit much, with me having to sort out the Plate, the Cowboys cricket, work, family life and this book. Thus, I had neither the time nor motivation to look at my fantasy league team for a couple of weeks, until the morning of the cup final. By that stage I was three points off the lead with a one-point gap to third. With the cup final completed, and thus the end of the fantasy league season, I finished second in 17,020th place overall with1573 points and, incredibly, only two points off the lead, the third placed man was a good ten points off us but still a mighty close run in considering the competition is over 40 weeks and so many points were scored. Both Hansen and Branson finished miles behind me, and Hansen is watching football all the time, as his job, how embarrassing for the lad.

The cream on my football cake was delivered on Monday 28th May at Wembley. Due to the ridiculous situation of the ten-year 'Club Wembley' corporate tickets not being able to be sold for the day, thousands of seats remained empty whilst thousands of us fans (including myself and Ga) remained frustratingly locked out. Instead we spent a few hours warming up for the match with red wine and watching loads of old Derby footage on Ga's laptop. Into the Plough pub nice and early so that we could get the lucky seats from whence we watched the semi-final against Southampton. An exciting match ensued but Ga and I were in no doubt as to the outcome from quite early. We were holding them and creating a fair bit ourselves but on the hour unleashed the sheer talent that is Giles Barnes. It was from his cross that Stephen Pearson scored our winning goal. A tense last half hour but the final whistle was greeted with a good deal of hugging, shouting and Tequila shots. After five crummy years in the Championship we are finally back in the big time. Surely, even if we come straight back down, we should put ourselves in a tremendous financial position and be able to hang on to our best players and, perhaps more importantly, our legend of a manager, Billy Davies.

As soon as Derby began to get back onto the journalists radar, they began to stir up trouble. They have attempted to drive a wedge between Billy and the board. I don't think he will leave as he knew what he was taking on from the beginning and he has actually been successful in a shorter time period than was expected. It would be typical though for the rams. For example, we lost Clough after winning the title and we lost Burley after having the one good season in ages. Please do not add Billy to that list. The one downer that there may be is that towards the end of the match, it looks like Seth Johnson may have damaged his knee yet again, with all the fairytale stories surrounding Derby this season, will his tale be the one nightmare?

With Rovers joining Bristol City in the promotion party with their own play-off win; it was a heck of a weekend.

On a final sporting moment, just as this tome was to be sent to the publishers, it was announced that Bob Woolmer had not been murdered after all. One positive that could/should come out of this is the press hounds that push and push for a dramatic story, will have to take more care in future, as they may have forced the police's hands in Jamaica into making an early, perhaps rash and incorrect murder call.

With regards my family / home life, we have come a long way in one season. At the beginning of this journey, my wife and I were stuck in a relationship that neither of us could fully commit to. Since then, we have begun to fall back in love in an all-encompassing way. The future looks bright and we can live with our foibles. As a defensive minded player, it is no surprise that I am a defensive minded person. My first reaction to any fall out is 'why is it always me? Why do I have to change?' At least when we have a row now, I react this way for only ten minutes or so and after just one smack around the head I recognise what I am doing, take a step back and react in a more rational way.

As for that nice Mr Tony Blair, his season and his tenure is coming to an end. Of course, it is his tenth anniversary too, as Prime Minister. Whereas the Plate are in a stronger position than ever and will be continuing for the foreseeable future, Mr Blair's reign will be ending very soon. In 1997, Blair was in a position of total power, a massive majority in the Commons and the belief of the people. How could it be worse than what had gone before? Ten years of non-stop economic growth would also give him the leverage to really push Britain on. Blair claims many successes. On a macro-political scale I would rate Blair thus:

Crime: It certainly feels that crime has not been tackled at all. There are still very few police on the beat. They are only visible as soon as you step into a car and then they seem to be everywhere. A call to the fuzz with details of a crime provide nothing more than a crime reference number, no follow-up, no forensic detectives, no coroner who is hell-bent on solving cases. The main causes of crime: that a minority of society controls the vast amount of wealth thus promoting desire and jealousy, remains in full effect although this was supposed to be a Labour government. Also, the 'after-care' of the prison populace via probation services is incredibly lax. The jails are full, little money has been spent on this side of crime, so no matter how tough the sentences, where do you put the criminals and at best you simply have a holding station for them and no rehabilitation.

Health: Unfortunately, it appears that lots of money has been thrown at this project. The money seems to be diverted to bureaucracy and red tape and thus wasted. I for one would be more convinced by the apparent success of health policy if the government simply changed the definition of things rather than deal with them. For example, the waiting lists. The government claim that waiting lists are down but it turns out that this is mostly due to re-defining when the waiting starts.

The Nanny State: For some reason, Blair seems to have got it into his head that we really wanted the government to become our mother and tell us what to eat, drink, smoke and so on. The one good thing about Thatcher was that she at least gave individuals the power back to live their own lives. We are now spending untold amounts of money so that when you buy a massive cake covered in icing, you have a little sticker saying that this product contains sugar and should not be eaten as your sole nourishment. From July we will have to watch where we smoke. Not in the office, not in the pub, not in 'enclosed public areas'. Progress? I think not. Perhaps try to properly educate society so that we realise what we are putting into our bodies (if we don't know already) and let us decide, not some crazed, ageing, religious fanatic who couldn't even admit to inhaling a joint when a student.

Education: Are we in a position to do away with the nanny state because we are a knowledgeable and widely educated populace? No way. Class sizes do appear smaller. There appears to be a good deal of money in the schools system. Schools have been rebuilt. Exam pass grades appear to be high. However, we do not teach children how to think for themselves, to question what they are told, to look at the wider picture. Education now is a factory designed to have children take non-stop tests and pass them. Education by rote. Back to the Victorian era everyone. Plus we have the same old story of massive bureaucracy and red tape waste.

Immigration: it would be a simple problem to cure. Simply stand up to the press and say that we actually need these people. Once they are welcomed then they wont disappear into some sub-class. Once feeling welcome, the immigrants will be more prepared to pay taxes, earn their money, build our country and then return home, build up their own country and the cycle stops. By continuing the Enoch Powell rhetoric of the immigrants 'flooding' the country, Blair has done nothing worthwhile in this area.

Economy: Thankfully, the government gave more power to the bank of England with regards the economy. In consequence, Blair couldn't muck this up too much. The introduction of the minimum wage is one of Blair's greatest achievements. It shows an actual philosophy being put into action, against widespread condemnation. Pride and self-worth to the working class, whatever next? As with Thatcher though, who poured our North Sea oil revenues down the pan to achieve her aims, Blair has had ten years of solid economic growth with very little to show for it.

Foreign Affairs: Obviously, the single policy that will haunt Blair was his handling of the war on Iraq. War is an ugly thing. After the initial jingoism there will usually be a public reaction against wars' inherent brutality. However, there was very little sympathy left in the public's mind because we had been lied to in the build up to war. Simply removing an unpopular leader has never been the reason for war. 'Sexing up' dossiers, lying about the potential threat and then bragging that we are the lap dogs of the USA is not endearing.

Environment: Respect is due for signing up to the Kyoto Agreement and pushing the G8 into accepting climate-change onto the agenda. Let us hope he stands up to the mindless and selfish who would rather keep their weekly bin collections than actually have to recycle anything. The use of nuclear power is interesting as it shows that there may be a philosophy behind this rather than pandering to the press. Public transport is still in the hands of private companies who seem to think that: massive fares, standing room only, trains and buses, 'every now and then', with safety as an afterthought, is acceptable as long as the profits are high. I have not really seen a commitment to providing an acceptable alternative to car use.

Northern Ireland: This must be seen as Blair's biggest achievement. Every Prime Minister has a go at at it. Setting up agreements and plans and promises. Blair has had the guts to see it through; it seems with a great deal of personal input and effort. Although a different sort of terrorism has replaced one enemy, the Irish question has finally begun to be answered.

Style of Government: Certainly, Blair's government has not been quite as sleaze-ridden as previous. Whatever else we say about him, I thank Mr. Blair for the night of jubilation as the old guard were swept away. However, the backing of his cronies such as Peter Mandelson where it seemed that no matter how awful he was at a job, he would be moved into another lucrative post, was not pleasant. The 'cash for honours' investigation rumbles on and leaves a nasty aroma around a Labour Party. There have also been the corruptions of politicians who worked superbly at local level, but once had hit the bright lights and temptations of London, couldn't hack it. Stand up the likes of Blunkett. My biggest bugbear is the whole 'Presentation over substance'. Blair looked a capable man partly because he ran the government as a near-tyranny. The ideas of the tightly knit Blairites would dictate policy and if you don't agree then you lose the chance of ever having a top job. If one has no input into the deciding of policy then you cannot talk about it with any depth or knowledge or be able to see the long-term goal. We are left with a few MPs who are 'in the know' and the rest are left floundering and only able to say how wonderful Tony Blair is. This will lead to knee jerk reactions whenever the press question anything, and the public haven't a clue as to what is actually going on, therefore, any minor fly in the ointment will be seen as a disaster and the policy will have to be jettisoned (not a cheap option).

My dear old dad used to say that it didn't matter who the Prime Minister was, it is always up to the individual to make as good a life for themselves as they can, whatever the political circumstances. So now I will look at Blair's reign from a micro angle, that is, the affect on my immediate surroundings.

Crime: According to neighbours, this area is a lot better off than five years ago. I have seen or heard very little in the way of crime just outside my door. I am aware that for much of the local youth, the police are viewed as a stupid enemy and much of their daily lives seems to be based around drug-dealing and almost constant violence of one form or another.

Health: It is very rare to get a GP appointment on the day one is ill. We have lost an A & E department. There have been few moves towards a holistic method of treatment, just the same old medicate and vaccinate policy. We know how I have been directly affected by health policy and that is for me to lose my yearly grade pay rise and not to receive a cost of living rise this year. The mental health sector in general appears to be under incredible stress in Bristol at this time. However, we do have a brand new leisure centre as a new resource for the community. Unfortunately, this costs money, land that was free to use for any sporting-related activities continues to be lost at an alarming rate.

Education: The local Comprehensive school has been knocked down and completely rebuilt. The local primary school has more teaching assistants. Although my step twins are only in year one, the pressure is on them straight away. They have been tested twice and any absences are leapt on. When the twins began their reception year, there were problems with bullying. These seem to have died down a little which, I believe, shows that this intolerant and ignorant behaviour is coming from the parents and not bred on the playground.

Immigration: The Polish invasion is the most notable one in my lifetime. Somalians and so on, tend to stay in one community and you either live there and notice them, or you don't and you don't. The Poles are seemingly everywhere. In my work I hear every day that if one wants a house-move or a job or more money then you just have to put boot polish on your face. Every day there are moans about the Poles. There is no moral or philosophical lead from Blair and his cronies, tolerant and informed sources such as The Sun are instead left to whip people into a frenzy. Try and make a policy of their rantings.

Environment: We receive the bi-weekly refuse collection service. It was hard at first, especially with three children, nappies and so on. We got used to it, and now it does give a great deal of satisfaction to be doing one's bit for the planet. In fact, we now see campaigns for less packaging emerge. We have also witnessed the renovations of every single council property in this area. With the upcoming building of social and private housing, the future looks brighter for this area; there have not been many governments that have been able to say that.

Economy: As a three child family with the emphasis firmly on nurturing and spending quality time with our kids, and hence not simply chasing the money, the Working & Family Tax Credits have been a marvellous idea. As this is a Gordon Brown rather than Blair idea this would explain why there seems to be some depth and actual philosophy. A method of redistributing income and wealth to struggling families rather than the more blanket approach of taxing the heck out of the rich to feed the poor as in 'Old Labour' days.

At least the Plate can say that their tenth year cemented the positives about playing for a Sunday morning team that is committed to playing football as it should be and continuing to provide a community for waifs and strays who need the company of other men in a competitive but ultimately loving surrounding. Touch wood there will be many more for me to 'enjoy'.

www.ingramcontent.com/pod-product-compliance
Ingram Content Group UK Ltd.
Pitfield, Milton Keynes, MK11 3LW, UK
UKHW020132250726
13967UKWH00002B/602